Reading Strategies and their Assessment

Ronald Fyfe and Evelyn Mitchell

NFER-NELSON

Published by The NFER-NELSON Publishing Company Ltd.,
Darville House, 2 Oxford Road East,
Windsor, Berkshire SL4 1DF

and

242 Cherry Street, Philadelphia, PA 19106–1906.
Tel: (215) 238 0939. Telex: 244489.

First Published 1985
© 1985, Ronald Fyfe and Evelyn Mitchell

Library of Congress Cataloging in Publication

Phototypeset by David John (Services) Ltd, Maidenhead, Berks.

Printed in Great Britain by A. Wheaton & Co. Ltd., Exeter

ISBN 0–7005–1004–4
Code 8196 02 1

The project Formative Assessment of Reading Strategies in Secondary
Schools (Research Project H/140/13) was funded by the Scottish Education
Department and directed by Dr R. Fyfe. It was based at Aberdeen College
of Education from 1980 to 1983.

In addition to the director, the members of the project team were:

Evelyn Mitchell, Research Assistant
David J. Northcroft, Head of English Department
William N. MacPhillimy, Lecturer in Educational Psychology
Donald C. Cunningham, Lecturer in English
Penelope Algie, Secretary

Contents

Preface

In 1977 two reports were published which recommended major changes in the third and fourth years of secondary education in Scotland. The Munn Report (S.E.D., 1977a) proposed a new framework for the curriculum based on eight modes of activity or areas of learning. The Dunning Report (S.E.D., 1977b) suggested changes in assessment, and argued that national certification should be available to pupils of *all* levels of ability. It proposed three levels of certification: Foundation, General and Credit.

As a result of these reports, several schools throughout Scotland were asked to participate in pilot studies to develop Foundation Level courses. At the same time, the Scottish Education Department set up an extensive research and development programme to support this work. As part of that programme, a project was set up at Aberdeen College of Education to study the Formative Assessment of Reading Strategies in Secondary Schools. It is the work of this project which is reported here.

The project remit was to lay the foundations of a resource for teachers to use in the formative assessment of reading strategies. Particular attention was to be paid to the needs of teachers developing Foundation Level courses in English (S.E.D., 1981). A principal aim of these courses is to ensure that pupils have a secure grasp of the fundamental skills and strategies involved in speaking, listening, writing and reading.

Several of the investigations undertaken in the project are summarised in the pages which follow. These investigations were described in greater detail in the Working Papers listed in Appendix 1. Although the project was funded by the Scottish Education Department, the views expressed here are those of the research team.

Acknowledgements

The project team is grateful to the Scottish Education Department for funding the project and to H.M.I. Mr W. Nicol of the Research and Intelligence Unit for his support and encouragement.

Throughout the three years' duration of the project, the members of the research team were given valuable support and guidance by an Advisory Committee set up to oversee the project. The members of the Committee were H.M.I. Mr James Alison (member from 1982), Dr Sally Brown (Research and Intelligence Unit, Scottish Education Department), H.M.I. Mr Quentin Cramb (member until 1982), Miss Celia Craig (Principal Teacher of English, Westhill Academy), Mrs Margaret Eleftheriou (Principal Teacher of English, Bankhead Academy), Mr William Fordyce (Depute Director of Education, Grampian Region), Mr Peter Kimber (Senior Examination Officer, Scottish Examinations Board), Professor J. Nisbet, Chairman (Department of Education, Aberdeen University), and Mr Sydney Smyth (Director, Scottish Curriculum Development Service, Edinburgh Centre). In addition to his duties as chairman, Professor Nisbet gave invaluable advice on the practical running of the project.

The studies carried out in the project were based on texts and reading tasks representative of those used by schools piloting Foundation Level English courses. We are grateful to the Principal Teachers of English in these pilot schools, who readily supplied us with copies of the materials they used and with the detailed syllabus notes they had prepared for their departments.

A project such as this must make use of a large number of texts. We would like to acknowledge the assistance of the authors, publishers and commercial companies who allowed us to reproduce texts for which they hold the copyright. Only a few of the texts we used have been reproduced in this document. Many more were used in the individual investigations. A full list is given in Appendix 2. In this report, the dictionary extracts are taken from *Heinemann English Dictionary* (Heinemann Education Ltd.); the booking form used in Chapter 5 was reproduced with the permission of Thomson Travel Ltd.; the poems 'Boots' and 'Tommy Atkins' (Chapter 9) were taken from Charles Carrington

(Ed.): *The Complete Barrack-Room Ballads of Rudyard Kipling* (Methuen London Ltd., 1973) and 'Judge Somers' was reprinted from Edgar Lee Masters: *Spoon River Anthology* (New York, Macmillan Publishing Co. Inc., 1962) with kind permission of Mrs Ellen C. Masters. We would like to thank Calum Smith-Burnett and the Library staff at Aberdeen College of Education for their help in searching the literature and for their willingness to track down references.

We are grateful to the Director of Education and the Education Committee for Grampian Region for giving us access to schools to carry out the work of the project. Mr Charles King, Adviser in English for the Region, was enthusiastic in his support of the project and we thank him for his work in liaising with schools.

The cooperation and enthusiasm of teachers is vital to the success of a project such as this. We are grateful to those teachers throughout Scotland who helped us to try out our materials.

Many teachers made substantial contributions to the work of the project. The help they gave us took several forms: tolerating the interruptions to their teaching routine which inevitably occurred when investigations were conducted with individual pupils or very small groups, working with us in classroom trials of project materials and forwarding to us the data collected from trials they had conducted themselves. Their comments and observations on how pupils responded to the materials were especially valuable and led to significant improvements being made. We would like to acknowledge in particular the help of the following teachers:

SECONDARY SCHOOLS (GRAMPIAN REGION UNLESS OTHERWISE INDICATED)
Mr R. Caie, Mrs M. Dutch, Mr D. Ritchie (Aberdeen Grammar School)
Miss M. Dowie (Auchmuty High School, Fife Region)
Mrs A. Pickard (Banff Academy)
Mrs M. Eleftheriou, Mr J. Leiper, Mrs A. Robertson, Mrs C. Tyson (Bankhead Academy)
Miss E. Anderson, Mrs C. Strachan (Cults Academy)
Mr D. Pyle, Dr W. Donaldson, Mr R. Erridge, Mr I. Gibson, Mrs J. Milne, Mrs L. Scott (Dyce Academy)
Mr R. Bennett, Mr R. Adams, Mr A. Gibb (Elgin Academy)
Mr J. Dugdale, Mr I. Hamilton, Mrs J. Ross (Elgin High School)

Mr D. Cockburn, Mrs J. Black (Inverurie Academy)
Mrs R. McLeod (Linksfield Academy)
Mr W.G. McPherson (Lossiemouth High School)
Mrs M. Jolly, Mr A. Lawrie, Mr A. MacDonald, Mrs K. Mathers
(Mackie Academy)
Mr D. Bruce (Mearns Academy)
Mr J. Johnson, Mrs M. Raymond, Mr N. Stewart (Mintlaw
Academy)
Mr R. Caie, Mrs H. Matthews (Northfield Academy)
Mrs P.E. Craig (Peterhead Academy)
Mr E. Scott, Mr B. Ross (Speyside High School)
Miss C. Craig, Mrs M. McLay (Westhill Academy)

PRIMARY SCHOOLS (GRAMPIAN REGION)
Mr J.A. Couper, headteacher, Mrs B. Brand, Mr A. Cormack
(Cloverfield)
Mr D. Taylor, headteacher, Mr J. Anderson (Cults)
Mr D. Thomson, headteacher, Mr K. McIntyre (Elrick, Westhill)
Mr W. Pirie, headteacher, Mrs E. Owen (Tillydrone)
Mr D.J. Birse, headteacher, Mrs B. Edwards, Mrs J. Horsfall
(Upper Westfield)

In Aberdeen College of Education, Irene McDougall, Ian
Gordon, John Thwaites and their students helped us to try out
some of our ideas. Ralph Dutch carried out a review of the
literature on profiling systems on our behalf. We are grateful to all
of them for their assistance.

We acknowledge the valuable assistance given by the following
members of the College staff who were involved with the project
throughout its duration: Morag Taggart (Graphics), Alexander
Porter (Reprographics), Alison Kennedy, Lecturer in Computer
Education (Adviser in Computing for the Project), Susan Jackson
and Aileen Matthew (Computer Programming), and Keitha
Henderson, Mary Findlay and Brenda Sutherland (Duplicating).

Although this book has been written by two people, the work
reported in it was carried out by a team. We would therefore like
to thank our colleagues David Northcroft, Bill McPhillimy,
Donald Cunningham and Penny Algie for all their help throughout
the project. However, the final responsibility for what is written
remains our own.

CHAPTER 1

The Overall Approach

The aim of the work reported here was to lay the foundations of an assessment resource for teachers to use in assessing their pupils' reading strategies. The kinds of reading activities investigated in the research project are to be found in many areas of Primary and Secondary school curricula. However, the project remit required that particular attention be paid to the needs of teachers developing new certificate courses for secondary school pupils of average or below average achievement in English. The project itself, it must be stressed, was not concerned with certificate examinations.

It is useful to distinguish between two broad types of assessment. One type of assessment, summative assessment, is essentially concerned with summarising a pupil's performance in terms of marks or grades awarded on the basis of end-of-unit, end-of-term or end-of-course tests or examinations. This kind of assessment is usually quite formal and is separate from actual teaching in time and often in place as, for example, in the case of certificate examinations. Summative assessment is intended to sum up what has or has not been achieved by pupils at a certain point in time, normally at the end of a programme of instruction. Such assessment, however, seldom helps teachers to find out why pupils have been unsuccessful and does not explain why apparently successful learning sometimes breaks down at a later stage.

To acquire this kind of information teachers need techniques they can use to assess pupils' progress *while* teaching and learning are (or are intended to be) taking place. This kind of assessment may be called formative assessment. Although the term 'formative' is more commonly used in connection with course evaluation, some authors, for example Satterly (1981), have suggested that the term can be usefully applied to assessment. Just as the formative evaluation of a course takes place *while* the course is in progress, so the formative assessment of pupils refers to assessment which takes place *while* they are involved in a programme of learning activities. This type of assessment is not separable from teaching or learning but is an integral part of it. It is less formal than summative assessment and occurs during a course of instruction rather than at the end of it. It should help the teacher to gauge the level of understanding or performance that is being achieved and should also suggest appropriate action that can be taken if the level of performance proves unacceptable. It therefore has a strong diagnostic element. The emphasis, however, is on identifying difficulties inherent in learning tasks rather than on looking for learning disabilities in pupils.

The focus of our work was on formative, diagnostic assessment. Ideally this is an integral part of any sequence of learning activities. For the sake of brevity we use the term **formative assessment** throughout the report.

Two Conflicting Demands

Formative assessment aims to provide information of immediate practical use to both teachers and learners. Work on formative assessment, therefore, must relate very closely to what actually goes on when teaching and learning take place. It must be concerned with what happens when the curriculum is being translated into action. The logical first step in preparing a formative assessment resource was to acquire detailed information about the reading element in the curriculum. A large number of principal teachers of English throughout Scotland supplied us with information about the content of the courses they were developing in Foundation Level English. A close examination of this information uncovered a major problem which had to be solved before progress could be made.

In these English courses pupils were asked to read novels, poems, short stories, newspaper articles, advertisements, forms and so on. These were frequently presented in the context of themes or topics, which offered a range of reading activities similar in kind, though perhaps not in level of difficulty, to those which Primary pupils meet in project work or centres of interest. Thus, in one school, pupils working through a unit on 'Work' might be asked to deal with texts such as excerpts from the novel 'A Kind of Loving' (Barstow, 1960), D.H.S.S. leaflets and application forms, one or two poems by Philip Larkin, a telephone directory and a page of classified advertisements from a local newspaper. Pupils in another school working on the same theme, however, might be offered a completely different selection of texts. We noted that there was remarkably little overlap in the specific texts used by individual teachers even when they were working on the same theme. Teachers were free to choose the texts most suitable for their own pupils. Though novels were central to most of these units, there were no set texts. The range of texts in use was formidable.

Our problem was to reconcile two conflicting demands. The nature of formative assessment dictated that we work with actual texts that pupils used in schools. Yet the teachers and pupils we were working with were using a particularly wide range of texts. It was clear that there would be little point in preparing materials *exclusively* for use with particular texts. Even if we concentrated on a careful selection of these texts, we could not guarantee that the material we produced would be directly useful to more than the handful of teachers who happened to be using them. How were we to cope with this problem?

The fact that teachers used such a wide range of texts suggested that the texts themselves could not be of prime importance. Of greater importance were the 'kinds of reading' which teachers were trying to encourage by using these texts. It seemed that an assessment resource based on a consideration of 'kinds of reading' would be more manageable, and at the same time would reflect more accurately what teachers were trying to achieve. Our solution to the problem of reconciling these conflicting demands was to focus on *kinds of reading task* rather than on particular texts and on *assessment techniques* rather than on the production of specific reading 'tests'.

Describing Reading Tasks

An early concern of the project team was to construct a framework for the resource that was both workable and, as far as possible, uncontroversial.

An obvious approach would have been to base the assessment resource on an analysis of reading skills. We rejected this for two reasons. Our first reason was that no one analysis of reading skills or of the reading process has yet achieved general acceptance. There is agreement that word recognition can be distinguished from reading comprehension, although the distinction is fuzzy at the boundary, but there has been argument for decades over the existence of different comprehension skills. Some authorities (Davis, 1968, 1972: Spearitt, 1972) argue for a number of subskills (without agreeing on how many) while others (Thorndike, 1974: Lunzer & Gardner, 1979) claim that comprehension is a holistic process which cannot be subdivided. A project based on separable reading skills, therefore, would either have to make a key and contentious assumption from the start, or be sidetracked into a major effort to identify the subskills to be assessed. Interesting as this second prospect might have been, it could not be easily justified in terms of the project's remit.

Our second reason for rejecting a framework based on reading skills relates to what actually happens in schools. Foundation Level English courses are organised around the four modes of communication: speaking, listening, reading and writing. Similarly, projects and centres of interest in Primary schools are intended to encourage general language development. In classroom work, reading usually occurs in conjunction with one or more of the other modes of communication. Teachers do not organise their classwork in terms of reading skills. Thus, although at first glance it might appear appropriate to base the assessment resource on some kind of analysis of reading skills, this would not fit easily into the classroom setting.

The framework presented in Diagram 1 is used to describe reading tasks rather than reading skills. The term 'reading tasks' refers to what pupils are actually asked to *do* with texts during school work. We arrived at this framework after studying examples of reading materials and reading activities commonly used by teachers in classroom work. Although these teachers were working with different texts in different contexts, their aims appeared to be very similar. They were trying to promote competence across the same range of reading tasks. As we will see later, formative assessment often shows that pupils' difficulties lie not only in misunderstanding texts but also in misunderstanding what they have been asked to do with them. In electing to use reading tasks as the basis for our work, however, we were not taking up a position for or against the existence of discrete reading skills.

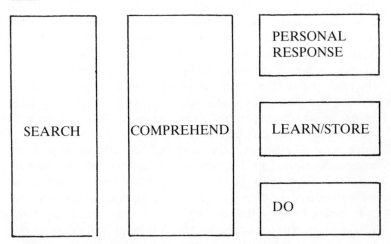

Diagram 1: Framework used to describe reading tasks

Our survey suggested that the principal component of most reading tasks undertaken in schools was comprehension. Although many reading tasks were exclusively directed at establishing comprehension, others clearly involved much more than this. Sometimes pupils were asked not only to comprehend a text but also to evaluate the text they had read, to relate its content to their own experiences, to comment on the emotional tone and attitudes adopted by the author and so on. In Diagram 1 we use the term Personal Response to refer to this aspect of some reading tasks. (Ideally we would want a term that is less all-embracing and that reflects both the cognitive and non-cognitive aspects of this kind of reading task.)

In other instances, reading tasks included a learning response. Pupils had to comprehend and then learn (i.e. commit to memory) or store (i.e. commit to note form) part of the content. This aspect of reading is of critical importance in schooling in general, though, paradoxically, less prominent in the teaching of English than in the teaching of many other parts of the curriculum. Other reading tasks required an action response and these we can term Comprehend-Do tasks. Readers are faced with this sort of task when they read directions or instructions and when they fill in forms.

We have used the term Search-Do to cover yet another important group of reading tasks. Frequently readers had to search for or locate texts or information within texts. In this kind of task, the *search* phase may be the main element in the task, as is the case when a competent reader uses a dictionary to check the spelling of a word. The search phase may be followed by a *doing* phase as, for example, on most occasions that a telephone directory is used. (Though understanding is also involved, it is principally understanding the nature of the task rather than the information found.) Of course, some reading tasks are heavily weighted on several elements. Using an encyclopaedia, for example, requires a *search* for the appropriate volume and the appropriate entry within the volume. It may then require the reader to attempt to *comprehend* the information in the entry and to retain that information in memory (*learn*) or in note form (*store*).

It should be clear from these examples that the components represented in the framework are not here equated with reading skills. Rather they represent elements of reading which have different weightings in different reading tasks.

The Project's General Approach

In terms of this framework, assessing pupils' reading strategies clearly requires the use of a *range* of reading tasks. This range will have to comprise tasks which have different weightings on the elements shown in the framework. In the project we could not hope to study more than a handful of such tasks in sufficient depth for our purposes. To increase the potential value of each investigation, therefore, we tried to devise techniques which could be used to construct assessment units for more than just the specific task in hand. Likewise, when considering the findings from a study of a specific reading task, we were interested in the possibility that they might provide more general insights which could be applied in the assessment of other, similar reading tasks.

We concentrated on three *kinds* of reading task, Search-Do, Comprehend-Do and Comprehend-Personal Response. Within these categories we focused on particular tasks selected as being representative of those which pupils are asked to undertake in the course of normal school work. Thus we studied Search-Do reading by investigating how pupils coped with telephone directories and dictionaries. We studied Comprehend-Do reading by investigating how pupils coped with sets of directions and with the problems of filling in forms. We studied reading tasks which have a heavy weighting on the Personal Response element by observing pupils' reading of two novels and a short story.

In general each investigation of a reading task proceeded as follows:

(a) after a study of the relevant literature, we attempted a preliminary analysis of the task and tried to identify potential sources of difficulty;

(b) in the light of this analysis, we devised techniques for constructing assessment units. These techniques had to be suitable for teachers to use in producing assessment materials for similar reading tasks based on texts of their own choosing;

(c) we used the techniques to produce assessment units which were then piloted in school trials;

(d) we collected detailed information about how pupils tackled these units, about the more common sources of difficulty inherent in the reading tasks and about what made items easy or difficult. In some instances we used this information to modify early versions of the units.

We can illustrate how this general approach worked in practice by outlining the steps involved in our study of pupils' use of a dictionary (see Chapter 3). We began the investigation by studying a number of different dictionaries and noting the similarities and differences among them. This information along with insights gained in an earlier study of a Search-Do reading task helped us to devise a series of possible assessment techniques. These techniques were used to prepare assessment units for use with a particular dictionary and the units were then piloted in a classroom context. We prepared a detailed account of the problems pupils encountered in these trials and tried to pinpoint common sources of difficulty.

The techniques used and the supplementary information gained in this and other investigations will be text-independent insofar as they focus on features common to a *category* of reading tasks. To the extent that we have managed to achieve this, our work on the use of dictionaries should help teachers to prepare formative assessment materials for use with other dictionaries of their own choice. In addition, however, it should have relevance for those trying to help pupils engaged on other Search-Do tasks such as finding information in an encyclopaedia.

Some Implications of this Approach

We have described in general terms how we set about developing formative assessment materials for use with different reading tasks. The approach we adopted had several important implications for the way in which the project was to be carried out.

The first of these relates to the role of pupils in supplying information. In constructing the initial versions of our units we simply had to assume that our preliminary analysis of the task was reasonably valid. Classroom trials, however, revealed weaknesses in the units. In these trials the most useful information came from pupils who had yet to master the task. Their problems indicated sources of difficulty which our earlier analysis had not uncovered. Though there was valuable information in pupils' written responses, even more valuable was the information which came from discussions held with individual pupils as they completed or tried to complete the units. Once they had committed themselves to an answer, pupils were usually more than willing to explain how they had tackled the items. Indeed, in some of our studies, pupils quite quickly developed a pattern of response in which they virtually dictated their explanations and comments to the investigator. Although we encouraged pupils to do this, it was never possible to guarantee this kind of cooperation. Those who voluntarily responded in this way seemed to perceive that there was a genuine interest in what they had to say. Supplementary information gained in this way was always examined closely in the light of the pupils' first responses. The data thus acquired were used to modify the units and to help in identifying difficulties. Pupils, therefore, have an important role to play in the preparation of formative assessment materials.

A corollary of this is that a resource for formative assessment must be conceived of as cumulative. More information will be gained each time units are used. Teachers developing such a resource will find it necessary to modify assessment techniques and assessment units and to augment their collection of information about how pupils respond to their materials.

The techniques we devised can be used quite informally. In almost all cases they can be implemented orally or with blackboard and chalk. Because we had to collect as much information as possible from as many pupils as possible, the activities in our units were presented in the form of paper-and-pencil exercises. Formative assessment as an ongoing classroom activity is usually much less formal.

Very early in the project we had to accept that if we were even to begin to carry out our remit we could not spend time polishing assessment materials to the point where data acquired in school trials could be legitimately subjected to a thorough statistical analysis. Our analysis of the data was qualitative rather than quantitative and, for the most part, the statistical approach was that of exploratory data analysis carried out as an aid to understanding the reading tasks and describing the difficulties they presented. Occasionally we were able to undertake a more rigorous psychometric analysis or conduct a quasi-experimental exercise. However, it was never part of our remit to produce psychometrically sophisticated 'tests'. Should anyone want to do this, then the assessment techniques would need to be explored further and the present findings would have to be treated as initial hypotheses for research and experiment. From the teacher's point of view formative assessment is *always* a matter of hypothesis formation and hypothesis checking. What we had to ensure was that teachers using the techniques would derive useful information from so doing.

In the chapters which follow we offer no more than starting points for the formative assessment of three categories of reading task. The units we produced are of interest only *as examples* of how the techniques can be put into practice. Indeed, where we have reported weaknesses in our own units we have not always gone on to revise them. Our aim was not to supply a set of ready-made 'tests' but to support teachers producing their own assessment materials.

CHAPTER 2

The Assessment of Search-Do Reading Tasks: Using Telephone Directories

Introduction

Reading is used for a variety of different purposes both in and out of school. This is reflected in the wide range of terms used to describe kinds of reading: responsive reading, reading for pleasure, reading for learning, reading for information, and so on.

There is a large group of reading tasks which we have labelled Search-Do reading tasks. The essential characteristics of such tasks are that the reader first searches for particular information and then acts upon it. Search-Do tasks very often involve lists or tables. The reader looks up a railway timetable and goes to the appropriate platform; he looks up an index and turns to the appropriate page; or he looks at the department store guide and makes his way to the appropriate floor. In each of these tasks there are two elements: a *search* element followed by a *doing* element. Search-Do tasks vary in the degree of emphasis given to each of these elements. In some of the more complex Search-Do tasks the reader may have to contend with significant additional *comprehension* demands.

Our work on the assessment of Search-Do reading was confined to two tasks representative of those in which readers have to use texts with a list structure. In this chapter we focus on a reading task where the emphasis is almost exclusively on the Search element, whereas in the next chapter we consider a more complex task in which the reader has to contend with significant additional Comprehension demands.

In our first study we looked at ways of assessing pupils' use of telephone directories. We chose to start with this because it was one of the tasks found in school curricula which had an easily distinguishable Search element. On the basis of our preliminary analysis of the task, we felt we could disregard the Doing element (actually dialling the numbers) since the reading demand amounts to no more than number recognition. Comprehending the entries once they are found did not appear to be a major problem either. What did need to be understood, however, was the way in which the directory is organised. An efficient search cannot be conducted without this kind of knowledge. We hoped that an understanding of the difficulties involved in looking up a telephone directory would offer insights into fundamental problems involved in Search-Do tasks in general.

The Approach

Sometimes assessment procedures require pupils to undertake activities – answer questions, fill in blanks, unscramble sentences – which are additional to or different from the actual reading task under investigation. Setting a series of interpretation questions is an attempt to assess a pupil's reading comprehension of a passage. Yet it is hardly a 'natural' reading task and is open to criticism by those who feel that reading comprehension should not be equated with the ability to answer such questions. If an assessment task differs too much from the natural reading task it purports to assess, then the only formative information forthcoming will relate to pupils' difficulties with the *assessment* task – not the reading task. Such information may, of course, be useful in modifying assessment materials. In formative assessment, however, it seems particularly important to interfere as little as possible with the natural reading task.

Accordingly, in our work on telephone directories pupils were asked to find telephone numbers (the natural response) and to find them in the complete alphabetical telephone directory (the natural text). Given these circumstances, we had to rely on careful item construction to give us genuine formative information. In an attempt to ensure that such information would be forthcoming we adopted two approaches to item construction.

1. In our preliminary analysis we tried to identify potential sources of difficulty in the task and to construct items specifically to probe these. This means that we did *not* randomly select entries from the telephone directory and set pupils to find them.
2. We controlled and systematically increased the complexity of the items given to the pupils.

These two approaches are complementary as can be seen in the account of the assessment materials that follows.

The Telephone Directory Assessment Units

We devised assessment units at two levels, with two parallel forms of the unit at each level. The 'Level 1' units were intended to probe pupils' competence in handling specific difficulties identified in the preliminary analysis. The 'Level 2' units presented more complex items constructed by the simple procedure of giving pupils only partial information about the entry they had to find. The task at this second level resembled more closely the task as it often is in real life.

In the assessment units the items were all based on business entries. We had three reasons for doing this. Firstly, in real life, people tend to remember or have a note of the telephone numbers of private individuals they want to contact. They are much more likely to use a telephone directory to find the numbers of commercial firms. Secondly, business entries offer a wider range of entry formats. Thirdly, when working with school pupils it seemed less intrusive into personal privacy to use business rather than private citizens' telephone numbers. Businesses exist to serve the public.

The Level 1 Units

In the Level 1 units the items simply consisted of the printed names and addresses of business establishments. They were laid out as shown in this (fictitious) example.

JOHN SPENCER, Slater
5 Hope Terrace, Old Insch.

Notice that the item contains all the information that would be included in the directory entry. Where words in the entry appeared in block capitals these were retained in the item. Pupils were asked to find and write down the telephone numbers of these businesses.

The units had several features designed to provide formative information about pupils' performances. Firstly, each entry to be sought appeared in an alphabetic section of the directory quite distant from the one in which the previous entry was to be found. This meant that pupils had to cope with the whole directory and not just a restricted part of it.

Secondly, the entries were to be found in surname lists of varying lengths. This meant that pupils had often to make use of the initial letter of Christian names to locate entries. Even adults hesitate before searching through a long list of MacDonalds for a particular entry. Searching for very rare surnames, however, is also quite exacting. We asked pupils to search long lists and also to find telephone numbers where surnames were rare, sometimes unique in the directory in use.

Thirdly, the items we prepared required pupils to deal with a reasonable sample of the more common entry formats. This meant that pupils had to understand something of how the list structure of a directory is organised. Few adults would be able to explain the rules by which entries are sequenced in a telephone directory. Most adults, however, do have an implicit understanding of these rules and it is this understanding which directs them to look up 'John Spencer' under 'S' but to look under 'M' for 'Marks and Spencer'. Similarly, faced with 'Robert Thomson & Sons', adults will look under neither 'R' or 'S', but under 'T'. The first 'item' quoted – 'John Spencer' – appears in an entry which is the most common of the three formats just mentioned. However, an assessment based entirely on this kind of entry would not be valid. Indeed, we have evidence to suggest that practice only with this, the most common type of entry, may hinder pupils when they encounter other types of entry. Formative assessment must therefore take account of different entry formats when studying how pupils cope with telephone directories. Only then can the teacher be confident that the list structure of the text has been grasped.

The Level 2 Units

The Level 1 task resembled the real life task to the extent that it required pupils to handle a complete telephone directory, not a specially compiled page or set of pages. Despite this, the Level 1 task offered only a few of the complications which can be met when telephone numbers have to be found in everyday life. To achieve closer correspondence with reality we produced the Level 2 Units. A sample item will demonstrate the difference –

"You need some more timber from Fleming's in Elgin. Which number will you ring?"

The item contains the essential information needed to find the entry but the pupil is left to select that information from the item as a whole. He must decide which word to focus on to begin his search for the entry. Later in the search he will have to use more of the information available in the item.

The Findings

The Level 1 units revealed two principal sources of difficulty:

(a) difficulties in grasping the list structure (i.e. knowing how the telephone directory is organised);
(b) problems of perception and memory.

The Level 2 units showed up difficulties of another kind:

(c) tactical difficulties.

At both levels we found that the pupil's performance was weakened by

(d) incidental difficulties: undue concern or puzzlement over particular features in the text, the understanding of which was not essential for the task itself.

We will look at each of these in turn.

1. *Difficulties in grasping the list structure*

Let us imagine that pupils who are unfamiliar with telephone directories are given absolutely no guidance as to how to use them and consequently have to learn through trial and error. How might they come to understand how the telephone directory works? We list here the first six entries in one of our Level 1 units. (In our items pupils were given all the information that appeared in the directory entries. For the purpose of this discussion we have concentrated simply on names.)

1.   JAMES G. BARRACK
2.   JOHN PARK (JEWELLER)
3.   ROBERT THOMSON & SONS LTD.
4.   BARRON & McALLAN
5.   THE VALLEY HOTEL
6.   CENTRAL SECRETARIAL SERVICE LTD.

Rather than provide a lengthy list of the difficulties experienced by pupils, we will try to demonstrate that pupils' errors were usually based on quite reasonable, though incorrect, assumptions about how the information in a directory is organised.

Faced with JAMES G. BARRACK, a possible approach, and one which several pupils adopted, is to check under JAMES. This approach is understandable but it will not lead to success. Two obvious possibilities exist: move on to the next item or try looking up BARRACK. Assuming that the pupils do choose to move on to the next items they will continue to fail with Items 2 and 3 but may achieve sudden success with Item 4 and again with Item 6. This pattern of correct answers, i.e. Items 1 to 3 wrong and Items 4, 6 and sometimes 5 correct did, in fact, occur. This shows that those with no knowledge of the structure of the telephone directory can get 'simple' items like no. 1 wrong, but can answer correctly items which often prove quite difficult for pupils who do have sufficient understanding to know that you do not look up first names.

What happens when pupils change tactics and look up BARRACK rather than JAMES on Item 1? They are rewarded with success. It is important, however, to establish what they have learned. Have they learned to look up *surnames* rather than *last words*? Items 2 and 3 put this to the test. Some pupils did look up the last words: (JEWELLER) or SONS. Others who started off looking for the surname but did not find it often reverted to looking for first names. This is a measure of the insecurity of their understanding. Occasionally they looked for SONS or LTD. This approach, however, was born of desperation. We think it important to distinguish between two tactical phases in the performance of the inexperienced. In the first phase, such pupils change tactics quite logically, although sometimes incorrectly. They may be looking for the correct word but simply fail to find it (see next section). When failure persists, those who do not give up sometimes move into another, more desperate phase where they will try anything. For example, in another of our Level 1 units, a pupil who despaired of finding *A.G. McGregor, Fish Merchant* under the name MacGregor started to search for Fish Merchant instead.

Pupils who learned to look at second names rather than surnames stumbled at Item 4 (BARRON & McALLAN). They looked up McALLAN. This item seemed to contradict what they had so laboriously learned in earlier items. Those who had learned to look for surnames now had to recognise that BARRON and McALLAN were two surnames and to accept the convention that the entry would be listed under the *first* of these. In Item 6, many treated CENTRAL in the same way as they would a Christian name and began a search for SERVICE.

From this brief description, several points arise.

(a) The Telephone Directory is systematically organised according to a consistent set of rules. Efficient users of these directories are unlikely to be able to give explicit expression to many of these rules. When they themselves are in difficulty, they operate on the basis of trial-and-error, which exhibits faith that there *is* a system rather than real knowledge of how the system places unusual entries within the list.

(b) The inexperienced user learns by experience that there are consistent, if complex, rules. If he fails to find a specific entry then he too resorts to a process of trial-and-error but, because of his inexperience, this process is not constrained by knowledge of the ground-rules. The errors made are, to a large degree, predictable and understandable. However, repeated failure may lead pupils into a wilder kind of response.

(c) Although no one would suggest that pupils should be taught a full set of rules, it was clear from our work with the units that the major rules 'tested' here, were learned by some pupils in the course of working through a single unit, and that these rules were eminently 'teachable' through planned experience. Perhaps learning that the list is systematic is as important as learning the system itself. Such learning gives the confidence to pursue a controlled trial-and-error search as opposed to a despairing, random one.

Even pupils who had a sound grasp of the underlying system (and had no problems in understanding where a particular item would be found), sometimes failed to find the entry they were searching for. This leads us to distinguish a second group of problems: perceptual and memory problems.

2. *Problems of perception and memory*

Some of the 'perceptual' problems were curious rather than of central importance. We had always expected that entries in long lists of the same surname would be difficult to find. We did not expect that entries in very short lists would also be difficult. In many instances, however, short lists were missed completely. Curiously, entries in bold type – commonly used for business entries – were also frequently overlooked. The pupils skipped over them and concentrated on the smaller print. This tendency would probably disappear with experience. Finally, in many instances, we found pupils writing down the number for the entry either immediately above or immediately below the one being sought. This was a simple error, but it took us a long time to track it down and see it as such. It was caused by a slip in the very last step of the task, but there was nothing in the pupils' responses to show this. The number they wrote down was simply incorrect. Teachers might be well advised, therefore, to take note of the numbers above and below the target number before carrying out exercises of this type, so that errors of this kind will be immediately apparent.

The memory problems are more interesting. The first problem was that pupils with a weak knowledge of alphabetic sequencing were at a disadvantage. Notice, however, that the knowledge required is more than being able to chant the alphabet from A to Z. What is needed is an awareness of the *relative* positions of letters and the ability to apply this beyond the initial letters of words. For example, it is important to know not just that 'Q' comes after 'O' but that it is comparatively close to 'S' and a good way from 'M'.

The second point of importance is that pupils did not remember the spelling of words accurately. For example, a pupil who attempted, and at first failed, to find BARRACK turned out to have been searching for BARACK. Careful attention to spelling seems critical in Search-Do reading.

3. *Tactical problems*

The two problems we have just discussed appeared when pupils were working with both the Level 1 and the Level 2 units. However, the Level 2 units revealed some interesting new variations on these problems. In these units we introduced items which directed pupils to entries which contained sub-entries. This posed the additional problem of having to cope with yet another list; a list within a list. For example, pupils were not sure what to do when they discovered that there was a collection of sub-entries for Radio Rentals.

More interesting, however, was the appearance of a new kind of difficulty. Some target entries now appeared within long lists of entries where the surname was identical. Pupils often displayed *tactical* weaknesses in searching these long lists to find the relevant entry. We will use the item quoted on page 15 to illustrate what we mean by this. There was a long list of Flemings in the directory. Having found the list of Flemings the most efficient way to proceed was to look down the exchange column and check only the Elgin entries in detail. This reduced the labour substantially. Unfortunately, it did not always increase accuracy. Some pupils who adopted this approach were satisfied when they found *any* Fleming in Elgin. They failed to consider the third piece of information and did not persevere to find a *Fleming* in *Elgin* who was also a *timber merchant*. Tactical weakness makes search reading tedious and may cause the search to be abandoned early.

4.   *Incidental problems*

In both units pupils experienced what we have termed 'incidental problems'. These did not derive from the essential nature of Search reading but were nonetheless important in that they hindered pupils or actually prevented them from completing the task.

Every author assumes that his or her readers will bring to the reading of the text a certain amount of knowledge and experience. The compilers of telephone directories legitimately make quite heavy assumptions. For example, pupils did not know that the word 'see' as in the entry

'Hydro-Electric — see Electricity'

is a direction to look up 'Electricity' to find the relevant number. Abbreviations also caused difficulty. Pupils did not know the meaning of 'Res' (or 'residence' when this expansion was given) and so could not distinguish business numbers from private numbers. Idiosyncratic abbreviations such as 'Drprs.', 'Bkr.' and 'Nwsagt.' proved especially difficult.

Conclusions

This study of the use of telephone directories suggested two major areas of difficulty particularly associated with Search-Do reading: difficulties in understanding the way the list is organised and difficulties in actually finding the entry. This second area can be further divided into perception and memory problems and tactical problems. There were, however, incidental difficulties which did not derive from the essential nature of Search reading. Though in one sense trivial, they were an important cause of discouragement and error.

Note

The telephone directory study was our first investigation into Search-Do reading. What we needed to do next was to check whether the two areas of difficulty we had identified were indeed inherent in Search-Do Reading and not confined to the use of telephone directories. We therefore undertook a study of how pupils use dictionaries.

CHAPTER 3

The Assessment of Search-Do Reading Tasks: Using a Dictionary

Introduction

In our second investigation of Search-Do reading we looked at ways of assessing pupils' use of dictionaries. Dictionaries, like telephone directories, are lists structured according to the alphabetic principle. The rules which govern how entries are structured are, however, infinitely more complex. A study of the similarities and differences between dictionaries (Mitchell, 1983) showed that similarities occur only at a very general level and that dictionaries vary dramatically when details of presentation are considered. This casts some doubt on the common practice of asking pupils who cannot find a word in their desk dictionary to look up another, usually larger, dictionary.

In the previous chapter we discussed a Search-Do reading task (using telephone directories) where the weighting was overwhelmingly on the Search element. Understanding the entries constituted a relatively minor Comprehend element which occasionally gave rise to difficulty. For example, pupils were unfamiliar with some of the abbreviations used. Reading was only minimally involved in the Do element (dialling the number). Thus, although the actual task involved three elements – Search, Comprehend, Do – the first of these was predominant and was the focus of our attention.

In dictionary tasks, there is again a very strong Search element. In addition there is likely to be a very significant comprehension burden in reading the actual entries. Even when the information within an entry has been understood it usually has to be transformed in some way if it is to be used to clarify the meaning of a word in a specific context. This constitutes the Do element in this task and reading is clearly involved. Thus although in using a dictionary to find meaning the Search element remains strong, dictionary tasks at their more advanced level are weighted heavily on Comprehend and Do elements as well.

In devising materials for the assessment of dictionary use we therefore bore the following points in mind.

1. Our study of the use of telephone directories had suggested two areas of difficulty which were likely to be relevant to a study of the Search element in using dictionaries: understanding the list structure and actually finding the entries.

2. Dictionary entries are much more complex than those found in telephone directories. In a dictionary a wider range of information has to be presented very concisely and consequently the structure of entries can be complex. For example, sub-entries, which pupils found confusing in telephone directories, are commonplace in dictionaries. In dictionary entries the reader will often come across information irrelevant to his needs. All of this means that the Comprehension element in a dictionary task may be very substantial.

3. Once an entry has been found and understood in general terms, the reader has usually to match the relevant information gained against the specific context in which the target word was initially met. This is a very complex part of the task and constitutes a Do element which quite clearly depends on reading.

One more point is worth mentioning. Search-Do tasks can be successfully completed by pupils operating at different levels of efficiency. The difference between skilled and unskilled performance 'cannot be expressed merely in terms of the end result of skilled activity' (Reed, 1968). To illustrate, a 12-handicap and a scratch golfer both contrive to get the ball in the hole. The difference between them lies in how to perform this task.

Similarly, there are many ways of finding the appropriate meaning for a word from a dictionary, some of which amount to little more than trial and error. This has important implications for formative assessment. We may have to distinguish between elements of the process which are *necessary* for an adequate level of performance and elements which are *desirable* to improve the level of performance. For example, an understanding of different parts of speech and an ability to categorise words accordingly is not a *necessary* requirement for finding meanings of words from a dictionary, but having this understanding and ability is certainly beneficial if the user is to improve his level of performance.

The Approach

In this study we again attempted to retain as much of the 'natural' reading task as possible. Consequently pupils were asked to use a complete dictionary. Using a dictionary to find meaning, however, is such a complex task that we had to study it in stages. Had we not imposed this degree of control we would not have been able to gather formative information.

All our materials were prepared for use with the Heinemann English Dictionary, which has a very clear and consistent layout, and is, justifiably, very popular in schools. In this study we worked with pupils who had not used this dictionary before. This meant that pupils were more likely to be conscious of how they were tackling the tasks than would have been the case had they been working with a familiar text. In this summary of our findings, each of the three main elements of the task – Search, Comprehend, Do – are dealt with in turn.

Unfortunately, there is no agreed terminology for describing important aspects of dictionary use. In certain instances, therefore, we had to invent our own terms. For example, we created the term 'target word' to refer to the word the reader is asked to look for in the dictionary. The lack of adequate terminology is a problem that arises not only in research work; it is also a problem for pupils handling dictionaries and for teachers training pupils in how to use them. For pupils the problem may be more than just a lack of vocabulary; they may also lack those concepts which make solving 'dictionary problems' easier. We are not suggesting that our terminology should necessarily be adopted by teachers. We do think, however, that teachers will need to have a set of agreed terms when teaching pupils how to use a dictionary.

Assessing the Search Element: Techniques and Findings

1. *How do pupils search for target entries?*

The first part of Unit 1 concentrated on the Search aspect of performance and simply asked pupils to write down the number of the page on which they found the target word. This approach eliminated the Comprehension and Do elements altogether. Pupils were presented with the following:

Below is a list of words in **heavy black print**.
Find each word in your dictionary.
On the dotted line write down the page it is on.

1. **dice**   It is on page . . . .
2. **tide**   It is on page . . . .
3. **maid**   It is on page . . . .

4. **folio**   It is on page . . . .
5. **sandpiper** It is on page . . . .

Even this seemingly simple task yielded interesting information and suggested four features of performance to be looked for when assessing pupils' work with dictionaries.

(a) ABILITY TO CHANGE THE FOCUS OF ATTENTION
    To be efficient, the focus of the reader's attention must change as the search progresses. In the initial stage, when the aim is to find the alphabetic division in which the word is to be found, a 'gross' search is appropriate. At a later stage a 'finer' search will be necessary. Inefficiency arises when pupils do not adjust

their level of search as necessary. We found that pupils using too gross a search level often missed the word completely. On the other hand, pupils who used a fine level of search throughout took too long to arrive at the target entry, tended to become discouraged and were tempted to give up.

(b) ABILITY TO APPLY ALPHABETIC SEQUENCING
The 'finer' level of search often involves applying knowledge of alphabetic sequencing at the level of the third, fourth or even fifth letter in words. This can prove very taxing.

(c) DIRECTION OF SCANNING
Efficient searching involves forward and backward scanning. When readers scan forward, first scanning divisions and pages, and then columns and entries, the direction of the scan means that they come across important information first and less important information later. The direction of the scan follows the structure of the dictionary. In contrast, backward scanning means that readers encounter the least important information first. In many instances, pupils who started scanning pages from the bottom stopped their scan before reaching the top. One disadvantage of this was that they made no use of guide words. A more important effect became apparent in later units. Pupils who adopted a backward scan first came across the target word as a sub-entry and often felt no need to check through the entry as a whole to find a more appropriate meaning.

(d) INADEQUATE ATTENTION TO TARGET WORDS
Difficulties can arise from a pupil's perception or misperception of the target word. Sometimes a search seemed to be governed by the pupil's pronunciation of the word rather than by its spelling. For example, in trying to find **dice** a pupil focused on words beginning with **dis..** . It may well be that by the time the pupil arrived at the '**di**-section' he was no longer operating on visual memory for the word but was attending only to the sound of it. It is interesting to speculate whether he would have performed better if he had been unable to pronounce the word. At other times pupils adopted a 'reading' rather than a 'spelling' approach to words, i.e. they did not

pay sufficient attention to the letter patterns within them and so misread them. For example, **sandpiper** was sometimes misread as 'sandpaper'. A pupil commented, "I just took a glimpse at it and I thought it was 'sandpaper' ". When words are presented orally rather than in written form (which might well be the case in real life) difficulties due to uncertainty over spelling are likely to be even greater.

Searching for a target entry, then, is not a simple process. Provided that the target words are carefully chosen much can be learned by observing how pupils carry out this first search. When this early stage has been mastered pupils can more easily move on to the more complex task of searching within entries for the appropriate meaning of a word in context.

2. *Do pupils understand how entries are structured?*

The Search aspect of the task does not end when the target entry has been found. The entry itself has then to be searched to establish that it is, in fact, the one which contains the relevant information.

A firm grasp of how main entry words are signalled and of what constitutes a complete entry is an essential first step in achieving an understanding of how entries are structured. In the second part of Unit 1 we tried to assess whether pupils were aware of the outer limits of an entry. (We felt no need to do this in our telephone directory study since for the most part entries are single lines.)

Our approach was simple. Pupils were presented with the following:

Below is another list of words. Find each word in your dictionary.
Look for the next main entry word. Write it on the dotted line.

Here is an example. It has been done for you.

perform   The next main entry word is   *perfume*
                                           ....

---

6. **limit**   The next main entry word is . . . .

7. **through**   The next main entry word is . . . .

8. **between**   The next main entry word is . . . .

9. **pull**   The next main entry word is . . . .

10. **class**   The next main entry word is . . . .

Notice the use of the term 'main entry word'. This is one of the terms we had to create and explain to the pupils.

Pupils' work on this second part of Unit 1 revealed the importance of recognising and making use of signals in the text. In assessing pupils' performances teachers should be alert to potential difficulties in handling two features.

(a) Pupils may have difficulty in identifying where one entry ends and another begins. We can take as an example one pupil's response to Item 10. The correct answer was **classic**. The pupil responded with **clatter**. He had bypassed **classic, classical, classicism, classification, classified advertisement, classify,** and **classy** which, for him, were not to be regarded as main entry words. All of them begin with **class**, the initial target word. Pupils who made this kind of error appeared to be applying the following rule: 'If a word begins with the main entry word that comes immediately before it, then it is not to be regarded as a *new* main entry word'.

(b) Pupils may not realise that entries can extend beyond the end of a column and so may finish their search before the end of the entry.

However, it is not enough to be able to recognise where one entry ends and another begins. Unless pupils have some appreciation of the internal structure of complex entries they are forced back on a time-consuming, line-by-line reading of the entry. In Unit 4 we attempted to examine the difficulties that might arise in searching within such an entry.

Pupils found it difficult to understand the basis on which an entry was 'chunked'. In the Heinemann English Dictionary entries are partitioned firstly according to part of speech and subsequently according to meaning. To direct pupils' attention to this structure we asked them to count the number of different parts of speech the main entry word could be used as. We had, and still have, reservations about using this approach and hence have not reproduced items from the unit here. We would argue, however, that some appreciation of how entries are structured, especially complex entries, is sufficiently important for efficient dictionary use to warrant further examination.

Assessing the Comprehension Element: Techniques and Findings

1. *Can pupils identify the part of a definition which fits a particular context?*

We turn now to the problems involved in dealing with definitions of meaning. Unit 2 provided a relatively easy, transitional task in handling meaning. Pupils were asked to complete a sentence by simply copying out part of the definition of a target word. In everyday circumstances where a dictionary is used to clarify meaning, readers would usually have to manipulate the definition to a much greater extent.

Here are the first four items in the unit:

Look up each word in **heavy black print** in your dictionary.
Read the meaning and complete the sentence.

1. **Lignin** is the main part of ....

2. A **trug** is a kind of ....

3. If you are **gullible** you are ....

4. **Orienteering** is a kind of ....

Notice how bare the sentences are. We felt (a) that more elaborate sentences might distract by introducing incidental difficulties (there are enough of these in the dictionary entries themselves) and (b) that a bare context would reduce the likelihood of guessing and increase dependence on the dictionary definition.

In the easier items in the unit, phrases such as 'main part of' and 'kind of' were echoed in the dictionary definitions which the pupils had to look up. Pupils' performance in this transitional task revealed that the following points should be considered when pupils are asked to handle meaning.

(a) THE EFFECT OF UNUSUAL SYNTAX

It is common practice in writing dictionary definitions to save space by omitting what are thought to be inessential words. This means that the syntax of the 'sentence' is often disrupted. It then becomes more difficult for pupils to use syntactic cues.

(b) RECOGNISING THE CORE OF A DEFINITION

Definitions of meaning quite commonly consist of a core element plus an elaboration. For example, the dictionary's definition of aspen is 'a kind of poplar whose leaves quiver even in a light breeze'. We would consider 'a kind of poplar' to be the core of this definition while the remainder is elaboration. Elaborations are intended in part to help to explain the meaning of the core. Because of this they are often phrased in more familiar or more concrete terms than the core itself. Perhaps because of this, pupils who were in difficulty were inclined to give undue weight to the elaboration in formulating their response. Thus to the item 'An aspen is a kind of . . . ' we get answers such as 'An aspen is a kind of breeze' and 'An aspen is a kind of leave'. Although these answers are incorrect, the pupils do seem to be making use of the parts of the definition which they understand. The next step would be to use that understanding to make sense of the definition as a whole.

(c) EFFECT OF UNFAMILIAR VOCABULARY

Unfamiliar vocabulary in the definitions caused difficulty even when the unfamiliar words did not actually have to be included in the response.

(d) USE OF THE CONTEXT PROVIDED BY THE DEFINITION
Pupils who did not understand part of a definition often failed to use the context provided in the rest of the definition to help clarify the meaning. When prompted to use this strategy, however, many pupils were able to complete the task successfully.

(e) USE OF THE CONTEXT PROVIDED BY THE SOURCE TEXT
Similarly, pupils often failed to make full use of the context available. In many instances, simply prompting pupils to look again at the source text was sufficient to help them overcome the difficulty. We will return to this point later.

2. *Can pupils select the meaning appropriate to a given context?*

Pupils who do not settle for the first meaning they come across but continue to search for a more appropriate meaning, already show awareness that a word can have more than one meaning. To be successful, pupils also need to understand how different meanings are presented within a single entry.

Unit 3 and the first part of Unit 5 were designed to assess the ability to decide which of several meanings offered is the most appropriate for a particular context. In Unit 3 each item was one in which the target entry in the dictionary offered more than one definition of meaning. Unit 5 was even more demanding in that each target word was a homonym. This meant that pupils had to search several entries to find the correct one. In many cases they had then to select the appropriate definition from within that entry. In both units the pupils were required to do no more than copy out the definition which provided the meaning appropriate to the context. We did not at this stage ask pupils to give an explanation of the meaning in their own words. This would have added a further response burden which might have prevented us from recognising whether they had achieved the more elementary, but still difficult, task of filtering out inappropriate meanings.

For each target word, pupils were asked to find 'the meaning that fits the sentence best' and copy it out. Rather than give a set of example items, it seems more useful to give an account of one pupil's handling of one item.

Item 8 'The secretary was asked to **page** the manager.'

page (1) *noun*
a) a sheet of paper in a book, etc.
b) one side of this.
Usage: 'the Battle of Waterloo is a glorious *page* in English history' (= episode).
[from Latin]

page (2) *noun*
1. *Medieval history:* a boy servant or attendant to a person of rank, especially one given education and training in knighthood in exchange for performing household duties.
2. a pageboy.

page *verb*
to seek a person by having his name called, especially in a hotel, club, business, etc.
[Greek *paidion* a small child]

Pupil's 1st response: 'a sheet of paper in a book.'

Prompt: 'What made you feel that this would be the meaning?'

Pupil: 'I thought it was that one because she (i.e. the secretary) had to write out something or something like that.'

Pupil's 2nd attempt: (orally) 'It's this one' (i.e. **page (2)** first meaning).

Prompt: 'Can you tell me what it is that makes you feel it's that meaning?'

Pupil: 'Because of "secretary" – and "attendant to a person of rank".'

There were two weaknesses in this pupil's handling of the item. The first lay in misreading the source text. In his reading of the source test he did not give each element of meaning its correct weight in comparison with the other elements and so one element, in this case 'secretary', became overpotent (Thorndike, 1917). From prior knowledge and experience, this pupil associated 'secretary' (in the source text) with 'paper' (which appears in the definition) and hence chose the entry for **page (1)**, definition (a).

The second weakness lay in a failure to check the validity of his response. It seems that he did not ask himself: 'Does this meaning make sense in the source text?' Neither of the responses he gave could possibly fit the sense of the sentence. They seemed to be based exclusively on what he knew about a secretary. Syntactical constraints appear to have played no part in his thinking.

Here is another example illustrating both these problems. Again, the pupil was working on Item 8. He selected the definition:

'a boy servant or attendant to a person of rank'

and gave as his reason for doing so the fact that

'A secretary is a kind of servant or attendant.'

Notice once again that, even though their responses were incorrect, both pupils were making use of the part of the source text which they did understand. This is an appropriate strategy but inevitably it will lead to error unless the response is treated as provisional and is checked against the context of the total source text.

Having read the source text, many pupils did not refer to it again. A typical, but ineffective, strategy was linear rather than recursive:

STEP 1   Read the source text
STEP 2   Find the entry
STEP 3   Look for a meaning

rather than

STEP 1   Read the source text
STEP 2   Find the entry
STEP 3   Scan the entry
STEP 4   Read the source text *again*
STEP 5   Study the meanings offered.

Often the only assistance these pupils needed was a prompt to look back at the source text. It is worthwhile checking on the following features of pupils' performances.

(a) MAKING FURTHER USE OF THE DICTIONARY TO UNDERSTAND
    DEFINITIONS
    Definitions frequently contain unfamiliar vocabulary. Pupils
    rarely of their own accord made further use of the dictionary
    to establish the meaning of an unfamiliar word within a
    definition. This was the case even with pupils who were aware
    of their own lack of understanding.

(b) RECOGNISING EXAMPLES WITHIN ENTRIES
    Definitions of meaning are often accompanied by an example
    of the word used in context. Pupils did not always distinguish
    between a definition and an example. This often resulted in
    the example being offered in their response rather than or in
    addition to the definition. The examples were perhaps more
    meaningful than the definitions. In one of our studies of
    Comprehend-Do reading we found similar confusion about
    the function of examples.

(c) FAILING TO CHECK RESPONSES
    Pupils often failed to treat an initial response as provisional
    and to check it against the context given. Willingness to
    validate a response against the given context is critical for
    competent use of a dictionary.

We have reported several difficulties which occur when pupils
are asked to select the meaning appropriate to a given context. A
general point which emerges is that when readers are
overwhelmed by the complexities of a dictionary entry, they may
resort to operating on minimal cues. If a word or phrase occurs in
both the source text and one of the definitions given, this alone
may be sufficient to prompt pupils to select that definition. They
have not understood the complete definition, but perceive some
kind of link between it and the source text. This is, in a sense, a
positive approach *when used by pupils in difficulty* insofar as the
alternative may be simply to offer no response at all.

In Part 1 of Unit 5 each target word was a homonym. In
searching for a target entry the pupils came across a collection of
entries, where the spelling of the main entry word was identical.

For example, there were three different entries for **list**.

At this level of dictionary task there were inevitably additional complexities to be dealt with. When the task reaches this level the following seem to become even more important:

(a) USING SIGNALS IN THE TEXT

Efficiency at this level of task demands that pupils make use of textual features inserted to help the reader. Features such as signalling and separating devices, the presence of explanatory words and phrases and the use of examples are intended to *help* the reader but may initially confuse those who are inexperienced.

(b) USING INFORMATION ABOUT GRAMMAR

Pupils who understood and could make use of 'part-of-speech' information benefited greatly in this task.

(c) READING THE WHOLE DEFINITION

Pupils sometimes based their responses on only part of the definition. Their answers would have been different had they read and understood the complete definition. They were too ready to respond on partial understanding.

(d) USING THE CONTEXT PROVIDED BY THE SOURCE TEXT

Pupils did not make use of, or made only partial use of, the context provided by the source text.

Assessing the Do Element: Techniques and Findings

Can pupils transform or manipulate definitions of meaning?

The task set in Part II of Unit 5 approximated more closely to what happens when a dictionary is used in a real-life context. Pupils had to transform or manipulate the dictionary definition of a target word so that the meaning could be merged appropriately with the sentence which acted as source text. Often, this involved modifying the source text. Pupils were presented with the following:

Here are some more sentences. Use your dictionary to find the meaning of the words in **heavy black print**. This time we would like you to write down the meaning of the whole sentence on the dotted lines. You will find that often you can't use the words exactly as they are in the dictionary. You will have to try to put the meaning into your own words, so that the whole sentence makes sense. You might have to change the order of some of the other words in the sentence.

Here is an example. It is done for you.

The joiner placed the wood in a **vice**.

The joiner placed the wood in an instrument with jaws that would hold the wood tightly.

1. His **retort** made the members of the group feel uneasy.

. . . .

The following were the most common problems.

1. UNDERSTANDING THE TASK

    When, in real life, a person decides of his or her own accord to look up the meaning of a word in a dictionary, the nature of the task is implicitly understood. In these circumstances, the word is being used in a fuller context than is possible in a short item. This may make the real-life task considerably easier for those pupils who are able to make use of context.

    Though the task in this unit bore close resemblance to reality, it did not and could not replicate it exactly. In real life it is seldom necessary to actually rewrite a sentence replacing a difficult word with a modified version of its definition. It is not surprising that a number of pupils had difficulty in understanding the task, or at least in remembering the various steps involved in it. For example, pupils sometimes elaborated the sentence without attempting to clarify the meaning of the target word. Thus, one pupil's response to the item, 'All the pupils attended the meeting **save** two' was 'The teachers of the school save two were at the meeting discussing the cause of vandalism'. Nothing from the dictionary entry was incorporated in this response, the target word was retained and there was no evidence that the pupil was trying to clarify its meaning.

2. OVERLOAD

This was a 'high level' task and as such it required mastery in handling the more elementary 'problem features' of dictionary usage which were assessed in the earlier units. Some pupils who were able to cope with these features when they met them singly were overwhelmed when they had to deal with several of them simultaneously in the context of a single, complex item.

3. TARGET WORDS WITH INBUILT DIFFICULTIES

Derivatives and homonyms are examples of what we mean by words with inbuilt difficulties. The difficulty with homonyms lies in deciding which of two or more entries is the relevant one. The difficulty with derivatives is that the target word may not appear as a main entry word at all. The relevant main entry word has to be generated by the reader. To take a very simple example, a pupil asked to find **rated** will have to generate and then look for the main entry word **rate**. He must then transform the meaning given to fit the source text. Failure can occur at any of these three steps.

4. GENERATING POSSIBLE MAIN ENTRY WORDS

To find a derivative in a dictionary the pupils had first to generate possible 'parent' or 'root' words. Their success in finding a derivative was also affected by how they pronounced it. If a pupil mispronounced a derivative, this determined, to a large extent, how he thought the 'parent' word would be spelled. This in turn influenced his search. For example, in the item 'The jacket was **basted** and ready for fitting' the target word was **basted**. Pupils were expected to generate the root word **baste**. One pupil, however, thought **basted** would be pronounced to rhyme with 'fasted', generated and looked up 'bast' and was puzzled to find that it meant 'a fibrous plant material used in making matting', a meaning difficult to understand in relation to the source text. Thus, although uncertainty over the spelling of main entry words would be expected to cause difficulty when words are presented orally, the same kind of difficulty can occur even when target words are presented in *written* form.

5.   FACTORS AFFECTING TRANSFORMATION OF A DEFINITION

Pupils' responses to Part II of the unit supported our contention that transforming or manipulating information on meaning so that it can be merged appropriately with the source text is indeed a high level task. To illustrate, we present several pupils' efforts to incorporate the meaning of **list** into a source text. The item was:

'The boat had a slight **list**.'

The dictionary entries read as follows:

> **list (1)** *noun*
> a number of things, such as names or numbers, set down or stated one after the other: 'I must make a *list* of things to buy'.
> **list price**
> the price of an article as shown in a catalogue.
> *Word Family:* **list,** *verb,* to make or put on a list.
> **list (2)** *verb*
> (of a ship) to lean over to one side.
> *Word Family:* **list,** *noun.*
> **list (3)** *verb*
> an old word for listen.

Now consider the ingenuity with which pupils incorporated the definition into their answers.

Adequate responses to this item were:

> The boat was leaning slightly to one side.
> The boat was slightly leaning over to one side.
> The boat had a slight lean over to one side.
> The boat leaned over to one side.
> The boat leaned slightly to one side.

Other responses were less polished but still adequate. One pupil handled the item by breaking his response into two sentences:

The boat had a list. It was leaning over to one side.

Another pupil introduced his own word to convey the idea of leaning:

The boat was in a slant, on one side.

Yet another added information not even hinted at in the source text:

The boat which was leaning over to one side (with the list) it has a gun in it.

Despite obvious effort, however, some pupils did not manage to produce adequate responses. One pupil felt she had to introduce something to cope with the idea of leaning over:

The boat had a rail to lean over (!)

Notice that even when pupils have 'grasped' the appropriate meaning they still have to integrate it with their understanding of the context. The pupils' ingenuity in doing this can only be admired and it supports the contention that comprehension is a constructive process.

Several factors were found to increase the difficulty of the task. We can summarise these as follows:

(a) the presence *in the source text* of other words that were not fully understood;

(b) the lack of correspondence between the part of speech of the target word in the source text and the part of speech for which a dictionary definition was given;

(c) structural complexity in the definition of meaning.

It must be remembered that the findings summarised here relate mainly to problems in using a dictionary to find the **meaning** of a word when that word is presented in **written** form. No attempt has been made to extend our study to include, for example, how pupils use a dictionary to find the **spelling** of a word which is presented

orally. Even within the narrow area we have investigated, we have only begun to explore possible sources of difficulty.

Search-Do Reading Tasks: General Conclusions

We have now summarised the results of investigations into two Search-Do reading tasks. To what extent did the second investigation confirm the findings of the first?

In both studies we found that pupils had difficulty in understanding the way the list was organised. In a dictionary, however, the entries themselves can be lengthy. The organisation of information within an entry therefore presented problems which we had not come across in the earlier study of telephone directories. In some Search-Do tasks, then, pupils may have to learn to handle two kinds of list structure. The book itself – the directory, the dictionary, the encyclopaedia – will be organised as a list according to certain principles. Entries themselves may also take the form of lists organised according to quite different principles. This feature caused problems in handling telephone directories when the entries for major companies or local authorities contained sub-entries. The problems were much more obvious in dictionary work where most entries contain sub-entries and where even those without sub-entries contain information listed in standard sequence. Understanding list structures appears to be fundamental in Search-Do reading when using texts of this type.

In both studies there were pupils who experienced difficulty in actually finding the entry even when they did understand the list structure. These difficulties arose because of inadequate attention to target words or because of tactical problems.

In the dictionary study, however, there were many additional problems not found in the telephone directory study. These arose because the Comprehension element and the Do element are much more heavily weighted in dictionary tasks. For example, the comprehension of actual entries proved, as expected, to be very demanding and selecting the appropriate meaning to fit a given context (part of the Do element) posed major problems.

These two Search-Do reading tasks were sufficiently different to allow us to explore the hypothesis that pupils tackling Search-Do tasks experience particular *kinds* of difficulty. Insofar as the tasks were similar, common sources of difficulty were found. The strong Search element gives rise to the same kinds of problem for the reader.

Search-Do reading tasks are very common both in school and in everyday life. Some of these differ in important ways from those which we have investigated. Pupils must learn to cope with lists organised on different principles. For example, both dictionaries and telephone directories are organised on the alphabetic principle. The Radio Times and the TV Times are lists organised according to the timing of the programmes. Catalogues and trade lists, on the other hand, are frequently organised according to category.

Another important aspect of more advanced Search-Do reading tasks is the need to generate keywords. Something of this was seen in the more advanced dictionary units on the occasions when pupils had to generate main entry words. In looking up Yellow Pages, indexes, encyclopaedias and other reference books pupils have to learn to generate their own keywords. Frequently, they will have to be prepared to generate alternative keywords should their first search prove fruitless.

Finally, there is yet another important kind of Search reading. This is seen when readers skim pages of running prose to find a section relevant to their purpose or to preview its contents.

Constructing Assessment Units for Search-Do Reading Tasks

We hope that the information contained in Chapters 2 & 3 will be useful to teachers who wish to prepare their own assessment units for use with telephone directories and dictionaries. To be successful, such units will have to be tried out in the classroom and be modified to take account of what has been observed. As we argued in Chapter 1, building an assessment resource is a cumulative process. Our work should be regarded as only a first step in this process.

In this section we offer a guide to the contruction of *first versions* of assessment units for Search-Do reading tasks in general. This guide is based on our experiences in constructing, trying out, rejecting and modifying our own units. We have tried to present it in general terms so that it can be applied to a broad range of such tasks.

General points

Search-Do reading is a convenient label for a group of reading tasks which might more accurately be described as Search-Comprehend-Do. Here the term Comprehend relates to that part of the task which involves getting meaning from the entry once it has been found. In some tasks the Comprehend element is minimal while in others it constitutes a substantial part of the task. For example, reading an entry in a multi-volume encyclopaedia is often the equivalent of reading an article in a technical journal.

Natural reading tasks usually involve more than one element and this makes it difficult to identify where a pupil's problems may lie. For assessment purposes, it is sometimes possible to present the pupil with subtasks which focus on one or other of the constituent elements. When this is done for formative assessment purposes it is important to check that, when they are presented in isolation, subtasks make the same demands on the reader as they would in the context of the complete task. If this is not the case then information gained will be invalid to some degree and may be actually misleading. In the dictionary investigation, it seemed feasible to focus on the Search element by introducing a subtask where the pupil had only to write down the number of the page on which the target entry was found. There was no reason to believe that a search carried out in this subtask would be different in any important respects from a search carried out in a more complete dictionary task.

Item construction

Formative assessment items are designed to help teachers to assess whether suitable progress has been made and to detect where the difficulties of individual pupils lie. Difficulties in a Search-Comprehend-Do reading task may arise in any of the three component elements and items can be designed to assess pupils' handling of each of these elements. The initial step in constructing an item is to be quite clear about which element in the overall task is going to be assessed. Having decided this, it is advisable to reduce the demands which the other two elements make on the pupils. To illustrate, in Unit 1 of our dictionary assessment materials, the Search element was under investigation. The target word was given and the pupil was asked to give only the number of the page on which it was found. The Comprehend and Do elements were therefore minimised. This is probably the simplest type of dictionary item worth considering.

For each element the demand on the pupil can be varied. With regard to the **Search element**, the amount of information about the target word can be varied. At the simplest level, pupils may be *given* the target word in full and without additional information which might distract attention. The task can be increased in difficulty by giving pupils several pieces of information and having them *select* the target or key item from among these. The target is, however, still presented in the form in which it can be found in the text to be searched. At an even more difficult level, pupils can be given sufficient information from which to *generate* the target or possible targets for themselves. (Library work introduces another complication. In our work pupils were always *given* the text – the telephone directory or the dictionary – in which the target information could be found. In reference work and in developing study skills pupils will also have to learn to *select* the appropriate source text in which to look for the target information.)

In relation to the **Comprehend element**, it is possible to vary the difficulty of the entry the pupil will have to read. The simplest items will lead pupils to entries which contain little information beyond that which is immediately relevant. These entries will be relatively 'uncluttered'. At the other extreme pupils, having found an appropriate entry, may find themselves confronted by several sub-entries containing an abundance of information. They may have to deal with several entries if more than one main entry word has the same spelling as the target word.

In relation to the **Do element**, it is possible to vary the demands made in the response phase. Pupils can be asked to do nothing more than indicate that the target has been found (for example, by writing down the page number as in one of our dictionary assessment units). At a more difficult level, they can be asked to copy out the complete entry just as they find it or they can be asked to select and copy part of the entry. Finally, they can be asked to transform or edit the information given in the entry so that it fits a given context or satisfies a particular request.

We have tried to sum up these ideas in the diagram opposite. The diagram is offered as a starting point for teachers who want to devise assessment tasks for other texts which take the form of lists.

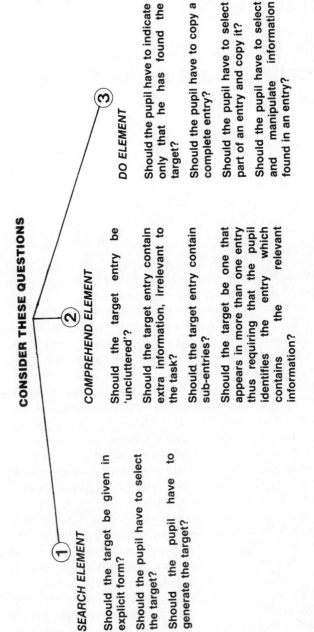

CONSIDER THESE QUESTIONS

①

②

③

SEARCH ELEMENT

Should the target be given in explicit form?

Should the pupil have to select the target?

Should the pupil have to generate the target?

COMPREHEND ELEMENT

Should the target entry be 'uncluttered'?

Should the target entry contain extra information, irrelevant to the task?

Should the target entry contain sub-entries?

Should the target be one that appears in more than one entry thus requiring that the pupil identifies the entry which contains the relevant information?

DO ELEMENT

Should the pupil have to indicate only that he has found the target?

Should the pupil have to copy a complete entry?

Should the pupil have to select part of an entry and copy it?

Should the pupil have to select and manipulate information found in an entry?

Diagram 2: A Guide to the Construction of Formative Assessment Items for Search-Do Reading.

CHAPTER 4

The Assessment of Comprehend-Do Reading Tasks: Reading Directions

Introduction

In everyday life we are frequently required to read a text and use the information derived from it to direct our actions. This is the case when we read instructions, where the directions are more or less explicit, and when we read notices (e.g. 'This office will be closed on Good Friday and Easter Monday'), where the appropriate action is implicit. In this kind of task a reader must Comprehend a text and Do something as a consequence.

Comprehend-Do reading tasks are very common in job situations. Sticht (1977), in a study of Navy personnel, reported that 60% of the reading tasks investigated were of the Comprehend-Do type. (The other 40% were Comprehend-Learn.) Characteristically these tasks involved the use of numbers and diagrams as well as text. In the job-situation texts usually did not have to be completely understood. The reader only required to understand the part of the text relevant to the specific task in hand. The reading materials commonly had a high level of difficulty. Two factors, however, compensated for this to some extent. The first was that the reading tasks were undertaken frequently, a third of them being repeated at least once a month. Secondly, the reading was undertaken in a natural context.

To complete a Comprehend-Do reading task successfully readers must understand the text *to the extent required* and demonstrate that they *know* what has to be done in response to the text. Failure to complete the task successfully does not necessarily indicate failure to Comprehend the text. The instructions may be inadequate or the Do part of the task may be beyond the competence of the reader.

In this chapter we report on our first attempt to assess a Comprehend-Do reading task.

The Approach and the Technique

The first example of Comprehend-Do reading we looked at was the reading of sets of directions. The directions we used were those found on the packaging of proprietary medicines. This is an important real-life reading task but obviously, in our study, we had to reduce the Do element to some kind of written or oral response.

The standard approach to assessing comprehension is to set a passage and ask a number of questions about it. This approach was not appropriate for our needs. We had to look for an approach that would resemble more closely what the reader has to do in the real-life task. Our solution was to provide readers with the directions from *several* proprietary medicines and to ask questions on only key pieces of information. This parallels what often happens in real life in that a person may have to read the directions from more than one medicine in order to decide which one is best suited to the relief of a particular ailment. The approach directed readers to look for the same kind of information in texts which presented that information in different formats. It also enabled us to simulate two of the characteristics of Comprehend-Do reading tasks reported by Sticht. Firstly, since we asked questions on only the important pieces of information, there was no need for readers to understand or even read the whole text. Secondly, just as in real life many Comprehend-Do reading tasks are undertaken frequently, the format of our questioning meant that the reader had to make repeated reference to the reading materials. Of course, the time scale was quite different.

The Assessment Units

The directions for using each of eight proprietary medicines were printed and presented on separate pages in an eight-page booklet. We had permission from the companies concerned to give fictitious names to the medicines. This ensured that pupils would not be able to rely on past experience of using a medicine whose name they recognised. They would have to refer to the 'texts' as they worked through the assessment units. We present extracts from our units to illustrate our approach.

For each item in Unit 1 we prepared a list of the (fictitious) names of the eight medicines in the booklet (see Figure 1). In response to each item pupils simply had to put a tick opposite the names of the medicines they selected. (At this point the reader may find it helpful to look at some labels from proprietary medicines. This should make the extract in Figure 1 more meaningful.)

Notice that in this type of item pupils have to look for the same *kind* of information in each set of directions. The pupils' ability to identify this important information is observed across all eight texts.

Unit 2 was concerned with another important piece of information. In this case pupils had to identify how each medicine was to be taken. Once again they were asked to do this across all eight texts. An extract from Unit 2 is shown on page 50.

In Units 3 and 4 pupils were asked to attend to several items of information and to integrate these. In Unit 3 this task is structured for the reader in that attention is drawn to three ways in which medicines might be used incorrectly. We asked pupils to shade in the appropriate box rather than tick something which is wrong. An extract from Unit 3 is shown in Figure 3 (page 51). The precise wording has been changed slightly in the light of our experience in working with the unit.

In contrast, the task set in Unit 4 (Figure 4, page 52) is not structured for the reader and, as expected, it proved to be more difficult.

Our assessment technique, then, directs the pupil's attention to the important information in a set of similar texts. We hoped that by using the materials pupils might be encouraged to focus on key information and ignore irrelevant detail. Although, in this study, pupils worked with a narrow category of texts, this reading strategy has a more general application and the approach to assessment can also be applied to a wider range of reading tasks

EXAMPLE:

There are **FIVE** medicines you could use if you had a headache.
Which are they?

Medicine	
PARVIT	
FARMAVELTONE	✓
GLEMORYN	
RELON	✓
PAMAR	
SILAPAM	✓
TROOVILT	✓
HYVANAM	✓

1. There are **FOUR** medicines you could use if you had influenza. ('flu).
Which are they?

Medicine	
PARVIT	
FARMAVELTONE	
GLEMORYN	
RELON	
PAMAR	
SILAPAM	
TROOVILT	
HYVANAM	

Figure 1: Extract from Unit 1

EXAMPLE: How would you use Parvit?

1. How would you take Farmaveltone?

Figure 2:   Extract from Unit 2

Example: A boy, aged four, has a dry cough and his father gives him two teaspoonfuls of Pamar at 8.00 p.m. and another two teaspoonfuls of Pamar at 10.00 p.m.

RIGHT

WRONG MEDICINE
WRONG DOSE
WRONG TIME

What the father does in this story is wrong.
Look in the booklet at the page which tells you about Pamar.
You will see that a child under the age of six should get only one teaspoonful of Pamar.

1. Your father has a dry cough and he takes three teaspoonfuls of Pamar at 9.00 p.m. and three teaspoonfuls of Pamar at 11.00 p.m.

RIGHT

WRONG MEDICINE
WRONG DOSE
WRONG TIME

Figure 3: Extract from Unit 3

Example: Mr Brown has a headache. He takes one Relon powder at 6.00 p.m. and another Relon powder at 8.00 p.m.

RIGHT

WRONG

1.   A three-year-old boy has a cold. His mother gives him a Relon powder at 4.00 p.m. and another Relon powder at 8.00 p.m.

RIGHT

WRONG

Figure 4:   Extract from Unit 4

and not just to other sets of instructions. For example, a useful exercise can be prepared based on a collection of classified advertisements for a particular type of product.

The difficulty of writing instructions that are clear without being too lengthy was first brought home to us when we attempted to write instructions for pupils undertaking these tasks. After several attempts, we concluded that the most sensible approach was to provide demonstration items to be worked through with the teacher's help. Different reading tasks do require different assessment formats, some of which will be unfamiliar to pupils. If we had had to depend on written instructions then we would have had to restrict our assessment formats to a few types which were already familiar to the pupils. Otherwise it would have been difficult to decide whether the problems which arose were due to the instructions or due to the reading task itself. In a project on formative assessment, the high degree of teacher involvement that is entailed in working through demonstration items is quite acceptable.

The Findings

In this section we report on the features of the reading task which proved difficult. Many of these are already well known in the field of Reading Studies, though perhaps not in the present context. It is widely acknowledged that specialised vocabulary causes difficulty for pupils in, for example, scientific or mathematical textbooks. Specialised vocabulary is less often recognised as a source of difficulty in everyday Comprehend-Do reading tasks.

We will consider pupils' difficulties under four headings.

1. *Coping with general statements*

Our evidence suggests that some pupils have particular difficulty in judging whether, or indeed in understanding how, a general statement applies in a particular context. Pupils may well appear to 'understand' a general statement in that they may be able to quote or paraphrase that statement in reply to a general question. However, when asked to consider the statement as it applies in a particular context it may become clear that their understanding is very limited. Their problem seems to be related to an important requirement in language communication: the ability to 'instantiate the general terms encountered in discourse' (Anderson & Shifrin, 1980). In most situations where language is used to communicate with others, people have to translate general terms into more particularised terms. Anderson & Shifrin quote the following sample sentences to illustrate the point:

> The container held the apples.
> The container held the cola.

Most people will instantiate 'container' as 'box' in the first sentence, but as 'bottle' or 'can' in the second.

The tasks set in Units 3 and 4 presented the pupils with an instantiation – of a word or a phrase – and asked if it was appropriate. For example, one set of directions tells us that the medicine in question can be used

FOR MILD SORE THROATS AND
MINOR MOUTH IRRITATIONS

This is the general statement. A pupil's question illustrates a problem over instantiating this statement: 'Is toothache (instantiation) a minor mouth irritation (general term)?' This is the kind of uncertainty which pupils often reported. In assessing pupils' understanding of general statements, they must be asked to apply them to novel situations rather than simply to restate them.

Why should there be difficulty over instantiation? There appear to be two sources of difficulty. To make successful instantiations pupils require, first, the appropriate background knowledge on which to base inferences and, second, a willingness actually to make these inferences. Both these develop over time. Pupils who are capable of making inferences do not always do so spontaneously. Anderson & Shifrin suggest that instantiation skills can be taught, basically through practice on selected materials. In spoken conversation instantiations are easier to make because the context is richer.

2.   *Coping with non-redundant text*

Directions are usually kept as short as possible because people tend not to read lengthy instructions. Directions on medicine packaging are further constrained in that they often have to be squeezed into a comparatively small space. (Manufacturers of medical products have also to ensure that their labelling conforms to standards laid down by the authorities.) All of this affects the comprehension task which the reader is faced with, for the texts are usually non-redundant or have a low level of redundancy. This means that all the words in a 'sentence' need to be processed. Deletion of a few words or even just one word may make sections of the text completely unintelligible. Fortunately, complete understanding of all parts of a set of instructions is not always required. Nonetheless readers have very few context cues to help them.

This may help to explain why certain words seemed to draw the pupils' attention and dominate their understanding. Thorndike (1917) called this the 'overpotency' effect. He found that some of the errors pupils produced in his paragraph comprehension tests were best explained in terms of the reader allowing the meaning of one word or phrase to dominate understanding of a complete section of text. It is interesting to note that a modern critique has described one of Thorndike's test passages as a 'mutinous conundrum' (Stauffer, 1971). It is a very concise single sentence paragraph, with little or no redundancy. Faced with a very difficult, non-redundant text pupils may have to base much of their understanding on isolated, familiar words, without the benefit of context to shape their interpretation of them. Text difficulty and non-redundancy may, therefore, be factors in *producing* Thorndike's overpotency effect.

3. *Coping with specialised vocabulary*

Technical vocabulary is a prominent feature in all the medicine labels. Words like, for example, 'febrile' and 'lesion' are highly specialised. Our questions were such that neither 'febrile' nor 'lesion' needed to be understood in order to identify the correct answer. Some pupils, however, got 'bogged down' by such terms even when understanding them appeared to be irrelevant to the task in hand. The more successful pupils did not stumble and get stuck when they came across difficult parts of the text such as lists of chemical constituents. Instead, they concentrated on parts of the text they did understand. These pupils seemed to recognise what was irrelevant or not important for the task in hand. Being able to do this seems in itself to demand a reasonable degree of understanding. How great a degree we simply do not know. What does seem clear is that pupils who do get stuck with specialised vocabulary in a non-redundant text will rarely benefit from an injunction to go back and read the text more carefully.

It was interesting to note that the pupils did seem to have a partial understanding of certain medical terms. Terms such as 'dose' and 'tablet' were familiar to pupils, but their concepts of them were too narrow and this led to some misunderstanding. For example, several pupils assumed that if the word 'dose' appeared in the directions then the medicine must be in liquid form.

At this point we should note that the presence of specialised vocabulary tends to make instantiation difficult. It would be expected that quoting examples of conditions which the medicine helps to relieve would aid instantiation. This was not always the case. Examples which contained unfamiliar specialised vocabulary tended to discourage pupils from making their own attempts to infer further appropriate examples.

4.   *Layout and incidental difficulties*

Despite the brevity of the texts, we found that this task had a more significant 'Search' element than we had originally expected. The layout seemed to confuse some pupils to the extent that they did not find the relevant sections of the text.

A number of the difficulties pupils experienced were due to misreading and/or failing to notice parts of the text. Many of these were similar in kind to the incidental problems reported in Chapters 2 and 3. We suspect, however, that the layout peculiar to this kind of text contributed to the increased incidence of such problems.

Besides being concise, the text is crowded together. Variations in typeface (lower case, upper case, bold face, italics, etc.) make reading difficult even in the decoding sense. These features may have been introduced by the manufacturers to draw attention to particular parts of the text. Often, however, they introduced inappropriate breaks in the text and distracted pupils.

Conclusions

This study of the reading of directions suggested four features of the texts which caused difficulty: the presence of general statements, the non-redundant nature of the texts, the use of specialised vocabulary, and the complex layout of the texts.

It is perhaps worthwhile making an additional point about the technique used in this investigation. The realities of classroom life dictate that pupils be set tasks which will keep them occupied for a reasonable amount of time. The problem with a short text is that often only a handful of questions is really worth asking. To produce an exercise which gives the teacher time to observe what is going on, it is tempting simply to set additional questions. We suggest that setting questions only on important information, but doing so across several passages, produces a worthwhile exercise of substantial length. Indeed the technique might be worth considering in any circumstances where passages are similar in structure and purpose but vary in detail.

Note

The study of reading directions was our first investigation into Comprehend-Do reading. What we needed to do next was to check whether the conclusions we drew were generally relevant to Comprehend-Do reading. We moved on to study Form-Filling as a second example of this kind of reading task.

CHAPTER 5

The Assessment of Comprehend-Do Reading Tasks: Filling in a Form

Introduction

In our preliminary survey of the content of English courses, form-filling was found to be one of the most common Comprehend-Do tasks undertaken by pupils. As a second example of a Comprehend-Do reading task, therefore, we looked at what is involved in filling in forms.

The connection between form-filling and reading directions is perhaps not immediately obvious. If, however, a heading is regarded as an instruction to write something (e.g. if 'NAME' on a form is seen as the equivalent of 'Write down your name here') then forms are simply sets of abbreviated instructions soliciting information. Forms seldom give direct instructions. For example, in the following extract from a travel agent's booking form, there

Departure Airport	Resort/Tour	Holiday No
Hotel	State hotel terms required B & B'fast, Halfboard, Full Board	

Figure 5:   Extract from Travel Agent's Form

is only one *direct* instruction, although four headings act as *implicit* instructions.

In considering the difficulties *pupils* might have, we were able to make use of recent studies of how *adults* cope with form-filling (Wright, 1980). We used this work to help us in our preliminary analysis of the particular difficulties likely to be found in the forms we intended to use. In the next section we summarise these difficulties.

Difficulties in Handling Forms

1. *Forms may present special language difficulties*

There are two reasons why forms may present particular linguistic difficulties. First, forms have a specialised vocabulary or register which includes, for example, phrases like 'delete as required', or words like 'applicable'. In addition to this, however, forms usually relate to quite specialised areas of experience which generate their own terminology. A travel agent's form will use words like 'resort', 'half-board', 'terms', and 'connecting flight'.

2. *Forms may contain different kinds of questions*

In a single form, a reader may have to answer several different kinds of question. For example, he or she may have to provide answers to free response questions, select answers to multiple choice questions and respond to a set of questions presented in

	Surname	Initials	Mr/Mrs Miss Master	Age if under 18
First Occupant				
Second Occupant				

Figure 6: Example of a Matrix Format

matrix format. Wright found that matrix formats were particularly difficult. In travel agents' booking forms something like the matrix in Figure 6 is quite common. To complete it successfully, the reader must use column and row headings jointly as instructions.

Even with questions of the same type, readers may have to respond in different ways. For example, in response to a multiple choice question they may have to tick a box (e.g. Male ☐Female ☐), score out what does *not* apply (Male/Female) or write out the chosen answer in full. The use of different response modes may make things easier for the person who has to lift data from completed forms, but it increases the difficulties of the person filling it in. This is a source of difficulty which should not be underrated. Wright provides a useful taxonomy of response modes and describes the difficulties which attend each of these.

3.   *The overall structure of a form may be confusing*

In tackling an ordinary text, the reader works from left to right and from top to bottom. Forms are not always so straightforward. The logical sequence in which the questions are most easily tackled may not correspond to their horizontal or vertical layout on the page. The form may be divided up into sections which are arranged in quite complex patterns. Readers may have a very real problem in deciding where to start and where to go next.

4.   *Forms may require information from different sources*

Sometimes a form requires only personal information and the source of such information is the person completing it. In other circumstances the reader has to read source material (such as a travel brochure or an information leaflet) before filling in the form. Difficulty in completing forms can therefore arise from problems in collecting the relevant information.

To sum up, the language of forms tends to be difficult not only because designers of forms favour a jargon of their own, but also because a form will reflect the specialised vocabulary of the area of life for which it has been prepared. Different kinds of question have particular problems associated with them and incorporating several modes of response in a single form will tend to increase its difficulty for the reader. The overall structure of the form may be confusing, and a form may require information from more than one source.

The Approach

We know a good deal, then, about what makes a form difficult for adults to cope with. It seems fair to assume that pupils will find the same things difficult, and that they may well have additional problems not encountered in research with adults. It would seem reasonable, therefore, for teachers to provide for their pupils a gradual introduction to the numerous problems that can arise in form-filling.

The most straightforward way to do this would be to present a range of forms graded for difficulty. There are, however, so many dimensions along which forms can vary that it does not seem possible to sequence a collection of them in a precise order of difficulty. Another approach might be to try to break down the task and focus initially on the Comprehend element, in the same way as, in our studies of Search-Do reading, we began by focusing on the Search element. In reporting those studies, however, we pointed out that such an approach is valid only when we are sure that subtasks presented in isolation make the same demands on the reader as they do in the context of the complete task. Bearing this in mind, we doubt whether a Comprehend-Do task can or should be assessed by isolating the Comprehend element. The most satisfactory criterion for deciding whether the Comprehend element has been adequately understood is to observe how the pupil tackles the Do element or an acceptable simulation of it.

In looking for a suitable approach to assessment it became increasingly obvious that there was no real alternative to asking pupils to fill in forms. Given the problems adults have in doing this, it was clear that pupils would need considerable help at least to begin with, and that different pupils might need different kinds of help. This suggested a possible solution. Would it be possible to get formative information about pupils' difficulties by looking at the level of help or support an individual pupil needed to succeed in the task? Teachers often use this approach in commenting on pupils' difficulties. They may say, for example, that a pupil can do a particular exercise if the instructions are gone over carefully, or if the difficult words are explained, or if only oral answers are required. What we set out to do was to use this kind of approach in a manner that was much more explicit and deliberate. The approach involves what Vygotsky (1978) calls 'dynamic assessment', the essential feature of which is 'to specify not merely that the child can or cannot perform a particular task, but to specify the conditions under which the child can or cannot do it' (Johnston, 1983). Obviously, to make this kind of judgment, we would need to offer different levels of support. We might then be able to identify the amount and kind of support a pupil needed in order to succeed on the task.

We decided, then, that we were going to observe pupils filling in forms. Formative information would be gained by examining the level of support which a pupil needed to achieve success. We now describe two ways in which it seemed we could offer this support, by expansion and by coding.

The Techniques Used to Produce Assessment Materials

1. *'Expanding' a form*

The greater degree of support was provided by giving pupils a preliminary task to be completed before they tackled the form itself. This preliminary task was to fill in an 'expanded' version of the form. Forms, it will be recalled, often contain single words or brief phrases which are intended to be interpreted as questions or instructions. Our procedure was to expand these into sentences which gave quite direct instructions. For example, if a form simply stated 'SURNAME' we rewrote this as 'Write down your surname'. In expanding the form, we simplified the vocabulary, wrote each item as an instruction and asked pupils to write in their answers. This meant that the same response mode was used throughout. Once pupils had gathered all the relevant information and recorded it on the expanded version they could then be asked to go on to complete the form itself.

Filling in a form involves gathering the relevant information and entering it appropriately on the form. Expanding the form helps pupils with both the gathering of the relevant information and the

EFFECTS OF EXPANDING A FORM

On Information Gathering

1. It gives explicit instructions about what information is needed.

2. The vocabulary can be simplified if necessary.

On Recording Information

1. The same response mode can be used throughout.

2. It removes doubt about where the response has to be recorded.

3. The expansion allows 'questions' to be presented in an optimum order not necessarily evident in the original form.

Diagram 3: How expanding a form can affect information-gathering and information-recording

recording of it. In Diagram 3 we try to show how the use of an expanded form affects both of these activities.

The language of forms and of Comprehend-Do materials in general is typically non-redundant. Expanding a form is intended to increase the level of redundancy to the point where the text becomes more easily understood. It may also be desirable to simplify difficult vocabulary. Technical terms, however, seldom have simple synonyms. For example, the word 'dependents', which often appears in forms, can only be paraphrased at some length and this cannot easily be incorporated into the body of a form. When preparing expanded versions, therefore, teachers will have to balance the advantages gained from simplifying vocabulary against possible disadvantages, namely the increase in the amount of reading pupils will have to do and the increase in the preparation time required of the teacher.

Filling in an expanded version of a form allows the pupil to gather and write down all the information that will be required to fill in the original version of the form itself. Once this has been collected, the original can be filled up by transferring the information from the expanded version. Though this transfer of information seems an easy task, pupils will now come across features in the original form which they will not have met in the expanded version. For example, the pupil may *now* have to cope with different kinds of questions and different modes of response. He or she may also have to cope with problems created by the layout. It is often difficult to know where particular information should be entered on a form or to decide on the optimum path through it. This led us to consider another method by which pupils might be supported.

2.   *Number-coding a form*

In preparing an expanded version an attempt can be made to identify the optimum path through the original form. The items in the expanded version can then be sequenced and numbered to lead pupils along this route. Clearly it helps pupils in the transfer stage if the item numbers in the expanded version also appear in the appropriate places on the original. We numbered sections on the form itself to correspond with the numbered items in the expanded version. Pupils then had to transfer the information recorded in, say, item 4b in the expanded version to the section numbered 4b on the number-coded form. Providing a number-coded version may in itself offer significant support for pupils whose principal difficulty lies in finding their way through complex forms.

Using the Support Materials

Fundamentally, then, we have two means of producing support to help pupils in form-filling: we can expand a form and we can number-code it. These methods can be combined in different ways so that teachers can determine how much and what kind of help a pupil requires to succeed on the task. Suppose several pupils are each working on the same form. Here are three *possible* levels of performance which might be determined using support materials such as those we have described.

LEVEL 1   The pupil is unable to fill in the original form. He or she is able to collect the information on an expanded version but still has difficulty in transferring this onto a number-coded version.

LEVEL 2   The pupil is unable to fill in the original form but he or she is able to collect and enter appropriate information on an expanded version. He or she also manages to transfer this onto a number-coded version.

LEVEL 3   The pupil has difficulty in filling in the original but is able to complete a number-coded version.

These descriptions of pupils' performances are phrased in terms of the support materials used. The descriptions will offer formative information to the extent that, by specifying the conditions under which pupils can or cannot perform the task, they enable teachers to identify sources of difficulty and to think about how pupils can be helped to cope with them.

Filling in a Booking Form: Assessment Materials

We had permission from Thomson Travel Ltd. to use a holiday booking form for Thomson Holidays Coach Tours in our first investigation of form-filling. We chose this form because it appeared to be one of the more straightforward booking forms. Furthermore, since it illustrated many of the problem features we discussed in Section 1 of this chapter, it seemed likely to provide a fairly severe test of our approach. An extract from the form is presented in Figure 7 on page 66. Because we had removed the form from its original context in the holiday brochure we had to make several minor modifications to it (e.g. references to page numbers had to be deleted).

Thomson Holidays Coach Tours
Booking Form

Thomson Holidays (Thomson Travel Ltd). Registered in London. No 837868
Registered Office Greater London House, Hampstead Road, London NW1 7SD

IMPORTANT Please help us by using
BLOCK CAPITALS when completing this form.
SHADED AREAS ARE FOR THOMSON HOLIDAYS USE ONLY.

Please give name and full details of person to whom all correspondence should be sent

Name _____

Address _____

Telephone No Daytime _____ Evening _____
(Emergency telephone nos for contact in case of operating difficulties.)

This form should be sent to your travel agent or to the Thomson Reservations Office with whom you made your original telephone booking.

REFERENCE NUMBER AS
QUOTED ON TELEPHONE

THOMSON HOLIDAYS
USE ONLY

S.81

Your Travel Agent†

Agents ABTA No :

ABTA

THOMSON HOLIDAYS USE ONLY

Receiver Stamp (Admin Centre)

Holiday No	Tour	Departure Airport/Coach joining point	Departure Date	No of Nights

Figure 7:　Extract from booking form used in study

2.   A.   Write down the name of the tour the group is going on.

      . . . .

      B.   Write down the number of the holiday.

      C.   Write down the name of the place in Britain where the group will join the holiday bus to start the tour.

      . . . .

      D.   Write down the date when the holiday starts.

      E.   Write down the number of nights the holiday will last.

      . . . .

Figure 8: Extract from expanded version of booking form

An expanded version of this form was prepared to help pupils with the preliminary task of gathering together the pertinent information. An extract from the expanded version corresponding to the lower part of Figure 7 is shown on page 67 (Figure 8).

When filling in a holiday booking form, there are two sources of information available to the reader: an 'internal' source and an 'external' source. The internal source is the knowledge already possessed by the person who is filling in the form. He or she will have little difficulty in providing detailed information about actual personal circumstances when the form is tackled in a real-life context. Pupils asked to fill in a holiday booking form in school, however, are not going to be in this position. This meant that we had to *provide* a context for the reading task. Pupils had to be given a set of imaginary circumstances which would place them in the position of a person who had to complete such a form. We therefore presented them with a short note or 'context sheet'. This explained that they were to imagine themselves to be over 18. (An under-18 filling in the form faces a complication which over-18s do not have to cope with.) The context sheet also specified the holiday to be taken, the date and place of departure, and so on.

Thomson Holidays Coach Tours Booking Form

REFERENCE NUMBER AS QUOTED ON TELEPHONE

THOMSON HOLIDAYS USE ONLY

S.81

Your Travel Ager

Thomson Holidays (Thomson Travel Ltd.), Registered in London, No 837868
Registered Office: Greater London House, Hampstead Road, London NW1 7SD

**IMPORTANT Please help us by using
BLOCK CAPITALS when completing this form.
SHADED AREAS ARE FOR THOMSON HOLIDAYS USE ONLY.**

Please give name and full details of person to whom all correspondence should be sent

(1A) Name

(1B) Address

Agents ABTA No:

ABTA

THOMSON HOLIDAYS USE ONLY

(1C) Telephone No. Daytime

(1D) Evening

Required Stamp/Admin. Control

(Emergency telephone nos. for contact in case of operating difficulties.)

This form should be sent to your travel agent or to the Thomson Reservations Office with whom you made your original telephone booking.

(2A) Tour

(2B) Holiday No

(2C) Departure Airport/Coach joining point

(2D) Departure Date

(2E) No. of Nights

Please indicate below facilities by ticking the appropriate boxes under room details.
Code: PB = Private Bath, SH = Shower, WC = Toilet

Meal Requirements

If your holiday offers a choice of Full Board or Half Board please tick your choice in the appropriate box below

| Room details | Mr/Mrs Ms/Miss | Initial | Surname | Age (see note below) | **(6)** |

Full Board   Half Board

Room 1 **(3A)**

(3B) PB SH WC

Insurance

Insurance premiums will be automatically added to your Final Invoice unless you fill in details of your alternative cover here

Room 2 **(4A)**

(4B) PB SH WC

(7)

Room 3 **(5A)**

(5B) PB SH WC

Special Requests

**NOTE ON AGES
Ages 2 to 11 years inclusive**: Please remember children's reductions can only be applied where the age of each child at the date of departure is clearly stated in the space provided. Children under 12 years of age can only be accepted on Tour and stay holidays

Under 18 years: A customer under 18 completing this booking form must also have it signed by his or her parent or guardian.

I enclose a crossed cheque/postal order to the value of £28 per person or £14 per child aged 2 to 11 years inclusive to cover the deposit for the holidays booked. I agree to pay the balance not later than 8 weeks before departure (such balance to be returnable in the event of subsequent cancellation subject to deductions on the scale set out in the Thomson Fair Trading Charter.)

I certify on behalf of the person(s) included on this form by whom I warrant I am authorised to make this booking, that I/we have read and agree to the Thomson Fair Trading Charter set out on page 7 (and the conditions of insurance referred to on page 8 where applicable) and that my/our booking is made upon and subject to those terms and to the conditions of all owners/operators of aircraft and ships on which I/we will be carried

(8A) Total amount enclosed **£**

Value   Cheque Date

(8B) Signature

Date

Signature Date

Signature (parent/guardian)

Thomson Coach Tours

Figure 9:   Number-coded version of holiday booking form

The external sources of information are the form itself and the holiday brochure. To make the latter more manageable we provided a greatly reduced eight-page version of the Thomson Holidays Coach Tours brochure, which we called the 'Holiday Booklet'.

On completing the expanded version of the booking form pupils were then given the number-coded version. This they could fill in by referring to the completed expanded version and transferring the information from it. A copy of the original form with code numbers inserted appears in Figure 9.

Filling in the Expanded Form: The Findings

Initial trials using the expanded version of the booking form were carried out with pupils from a Primary 7 class. The main features we had identified as causing difficulty in our first Comprehend-Do study (reading directions) were again found to present difficulty in form-filling. Even though pupils were working on an expanded version of the actual booking form, the presence of general statements and specialised vocabulary, and the use of non-redundant language all caused problems. Incidental difficulties, such as failure to notice instructions in block capitals, were again in evidence. We also noted that some pupils did not understand the function of the example which we included in Section 3 of the form. Their difficulties were reminiscent of problems with examples encountered in our work with dictionaries (see Chapter 3). We do not propose to discuss these in detail here.

However, pupils working on the expanded version of the form revealed new sources of difficulty. Three of these were particularly interesting.

1. Many pupils had an inadequate holiday and/or form-filling 'script'.

2. Pupils had to deal with more than one source of information.

3. Pupils had to make use of the 'imaginative' setting provided for the task.

1.   *Problems of inadequate 'script'*

Several of the inappropriate responses seemed to arise because pupils lacked sufficient knowledge or experience of what is involved in booking and going on a holiday. We have used the term 'script' (Schank & Abelson, 1977) to refer to the sum of a reader's background knowledge and experience which is relevant to a particular reading task.

In our experience it does not seem possible for anyone to anticipate fully the kinds of knowledge and the specific items of knowledge which are necessary to understand and complete a particular form. For example, some pupils who were filling in the form for a group of four or five persons wanted to have four or five rooms. They found that the form did not provide space for this. If they had understood that single rooms usually incur additional cost, it is unlikely that they would have decided that each person should have a separate room. The other extreme also occurred. Although the form allows space for four persons in each room, the Holiday Booklet does state that 'Prices are per person in a twin-bedded room with private facilities'. With more experience of holidays in hotels pupils would have known that the third and fourth persons in a room would most likely be children sharing it with their parents. It is rather unlikely that the form allows up to four people per room so that four adults can share a twin-bedded room, as some pupils seemed to believe.

Similarly, some pupils' difficulties stemmed from inadequacies in their 'form-filling script'. They had insufficient knowledge and experience of the technical terms and conventions used in forms.

2.   *Problems regarding sources of information*

A person filling in a form has to make use of 'internal' and 'external' sources of information. There are some items of information that only he or she can supply; e.g. names, addresses, ages, number of rooms required. In the real-life context this kind of information is determined by the personal circumstances of the individuals involved. On the other hand, there are items of information which can only be found in an 'external' source, in this case the Holiday Booklet or the booking form itself.

Some pupils had difficulty in recognising instances where they themselves were the legitimate source of the information required. They had difficulty in distinguishing between these and instances where they needed to consult the Holiday Booklet. Consequently some pupils puzzled over information which only they could supply.

'It says "Write down how many rooms you will need."
How will I know?'

On the other hand, some pupils supplied from their own resources information which should have been taken from the booklet. For example, the Holiday Booklet gave the number of the holiday in question as G4845 but one pupil supplied the number '1' while another offered '180'!

It may well be that our particular 'setting' for the task contributed to this problem (and we consider this next). Nevertheless it does seem that identifying the appropriate source of information plays an important part in this kind of Comprehend-Do task. These problems occurred despite the fact that pupils had been given time to familiarise themselves with the Holiday Booklet and had had their attention drawn to the relevant pages.

3. *Problems which may be due to our particular 'setting' for the task*

In order to ensure that the form-filling task would be relatively straightforward we provided a set of imaginary circumstances designed to avoid some anticipated difficulties. For example, pupils were told to imagine that all the people in the group were to be over the age of eighteen. This meant that they did not have to cope with the difficulties contained in the 'Note on Ages' section in the coded version of the form. Again, since pupils were told that they would join the holiday bus at Dover they did not have to cope with different holiday numbers for different regional departure points.

However, providing this imaginary set of circumstances meant that pupils had to deal with yet another 'external' source of information. Retaining this imagined set of circumstances was difficult for some pupils. One pupil who said he did not know the name of the holiday was prompted with the question, 'Well, which holiday are you writing about?' in the hope that this would lead him to look again at either the 'context sheet' or the appropriate page of the booklet. (Both of these gave the name of the holiday, viz. 'Five European Capitals'.) The pupil replied 'Wales'. The same pupil wrote 'Aberdeen' as the name of the place where the holiday was to start, and entered details of a nine year old as one of the holidaymakers. Thus he had not retained several important points of information given in the 'context sheet' nor did he seem to feel the need to refer back to it.

Filling in the Number-Coded Form: The Findings

Trials using the coded version of the booking form were carried out with a number of the Primary 7 pupils who had already completed the expanded version of the form. This meant that these pupils were supported in two ways: they could use the information they had already gathered on the expanded version, and the form they were now using was coded to indicate the optimum route through it. The pupils still experienced problems, as detailed below.

1. *Problems of perception and memory*

As in the Search-Do tasks and in our study of reading directions we came across incidental problems of perception and memory: failure to notice instructions given in block capitals, failure to 'notice' sections of the text and making mistakes in copying.

2. *Not making use of what was already known*

Pupils had the expanded version of the form, already completed, with them while they were working on the coded version. A number of pupils, however, did not make use of the information they had already gathered when they ran into difficulties. When prompted to use their expanded versions they were frequently successful. However, they did not spontaneously refer to it again when they were next in difficulty. Two comments are worth making here. First, in the dictionary studies we reported that pupils were frequently successful when prompted to refer back to the source text. Often, however, these pupils did not adopt this strategy for themselves with later items but had to be prompted again to use it. Secondly, in one of our studies of Personal Response Reading we found that pupils showed a similar reluctance to make use of information they had already gathered.

3. *Problems of specialised vocabulary and abbreviations*

Often these problems were inextricably bound up with the difficulty of coping with non-redundant text. Referring to Section 2B one pupil asked:

> 'What does it say in that box? – Holiday No?
> Do I just write Yes or No?'

'No' in the heading was not interpreted as an abbreviation for 'Number' but as an interrogative. Only in the world of travel agents would the phrase 'holiday number' be commonly used.

When filling in the coded version pupils were able to refer to the expanded version they had already completed. In it the potential vocabulary problems had been greatly reduced. It was clear, however, that the vocabulary of the coded version still caused uncertainty and puzzlement. For example, pupils asked:

> 'What's "Room Details"?'
> Is that (pointing to 'Tour' in Section 2A) Five European Capitals?'

Pupils will in the long run have to learn to cope with the specialised vocabulary of forms. Thus, although in our expanded versions we did simplify the vocabulary, we suggest that pupils working with real forms might be supported by offering them a simple glossary. We did, in fact, compile such a glossary for use with this particular form.

4. *Problems caused by the 'setting' provided for the task*

Though we had so designed the 'context sheet' that there was no need for pupils to cope with the 'Note on Ages', several pupils tried to struggle through it. This is a good example of how pupils will persist in reading material which is irrelevant to the task in hand. It is an even better example of how well-intended measures can lead to complete confusion. In trying to make use of the context sheet, pupils faced a conflict between 'actual fact' and 'imagined fact'. In 'actual fact' they were too young to fill in these forms and therefore required a parent's signature: in 'imagined fact' they were over eighteen and did not require a parental signature.

5. *Problems in coping with a matrix*

The sequencing and numbering of items in the expanded version and the numbering of sections in the coded version were intended to guide readers through the matrix. Pupils who disregarded the path we had worked out often got stuck. The results of this work with school pupils supports what Wright (1980) found in work with adults. Readers do have difficulty in finding their way through a matrix.

Filling in an Application Form

We undertook a second investigation of form-filling in which we used the form of Application for a Driving Licence. Since layout was unlikely to be a major problem in this particular form (the reader 'simply' follows the numbered sequence) we prepared only an expanded version in which there was some simplification of vocabulary. Trials using the expanded version and the original form were carried out with fourth year secondary pupils. This investigation confirmed the main findings of our earlier study. In particular it highlighted the importance of context in undertaking Comprehend-Do tasks. Real life provides a real context for Comprehend-Do tasks. When these tasks are introduced as a school activity, the context will, in most cases, have to be recreated by the pupil with or without the help of the teacher.

Conclusions

Those textual features which caused problems for pupils when reading sets of directions were also found to be sources of difficulty for pupils filling in forms. However, form-filling held further problems for pupils. Some of them had inadequate knowledge and experience ('script') to cope with aspects of the task. Some had problems in deciding which source of information to use to produce a response. Many had difficulty in accepting or developing and then sustaining the imagined context necessary for completing a form without the support normally given by the real-life context.

There is no doubt that the population in general finds the filling in of forms a tedious and unwelcome task. It is, however, an exercise which demands thinking and understanding. The techniques described in this chapter may help teachers to engage pupils more directly in the kind of thinking and understanding which the task demands.

Expanding a form, however, can be time-consuming. This is particularly the case with long forms although, once prepared, expanded versions can be retained and duplicated as required. It may be that in practice the technique of expanding a form is best used with comparatively short forms selected to introduce pupils to the complexities of form-filling. (Our reason for working with such long forms was that they incorporated a large number of the critical features we wanted to examine and so allowed us to collect a lot of information relatively quickly.)

Number-coding a form, however, is altogether easier to do and particularly appropriate with a long form which has a complex layout. We would also suggest that asking *pupils* to number-code a form (without necessarily going so far as to fill it in) may be a useful activity with diagnostic potential.

Comprehend-Do Reading Tasks: General Conclusions

In Chapter 4 and in this chapter we have reported on investigations into reading sets of directions and form-filling. Although these have been classified as Comprehend-Do reading tasks they are sufficiently different from each other to give an indication of the range of tasks which fall into this category. We hoped that the two studies would offer a reasonable sample of the difficulties pupils are likely to have with Comprehend-Do tasks in general. Our general conclusion is that forms and sets of directions have in common several features which constitute sources of difficulty for the inexperienced reader.

In the study of how pupils read sets of directions, we found that important sources of difficulty were:

(a) the presence of general statements which readers have to interpret in a particular context;

(b) the use of technical vocabulary, including familiar words which have a specialised meaning;

(c) the non-redundant nature of the text;

(d) unusual or complex textual layout.

The investigation of form-filling offered confirmation of these as important sources of difficulty, and also revealed that difficulties arise in Comprehend-Do tasks:

(a) when readers are asked to handle more than one source of information and to recognise the appropriate source to draw on for particular information;

(b) when readers do not possess adequate background knowledge and experience relevant to both the content and the format of the text;

(c) when readers are presented with a real-life text without the support which is naturally present in its real-life context.

Although the importance of these three points only became apparent during the second of these investigations, it is not difficult to see that they will probably influence a reader's performance on Comprehend-Do tasks in general.

Note

In the next few pages, we have tried to offer a general guide for the construction of assessment materials for Comprehend-Do reading tasks. We have to stress, however, that this may not do justice to the range of Comprehend-Do reading tasks.

Constructing Formative Assessment Items for Comprehend-Do Reading Tasks

In this section, we provide a guide to help teachers construct formative assessment materials for use with Comprehend-Do tasks of their own choice.

The teacher's first step is to check that it is in fact a straightforward Comprehend-Do task which is to be assessed. There are reading tasks in which teachers expect pupils to move *beyond* Comprehend-Do and to Learn or Store some of the content which has been read. Worksheets, for example, often contain Comprehend-Do activities which are usually intended to develop pupils' understanding of the subject matter and to help them remember it. Pupils, however, may perceive such worksheets as no more than Comprehend-Do tasks consisting of series of discrete questions for which answers must be supplied. Such a response is, of course, inappropriate if the teacher's purpose goes beyond Comprehend-Do. If, for example, a teacher wants pupils to *retain* information from a worksheet, this should be borne in mind when the worksheet is devised. A simple Comprehend-Do format will be inadequate for this purpose as it will not communicate to the pupil this need for retention. The guidelines that follow are for the construction of 'pure' Comprehend-Do assessment materials; that is, materials intended to assess simply whether a pupil has comprehended printed information and can act in accordance with it.

General Points

Just as some Search-Do reading tasks turned out to have Comprehend elements of varying degrees of importance, so some Comprehend-Do tasks had a significant Search element. In sets of instructions and in forms readers have to look for the sections of text relevant to their particular situation. A more accurate label, then, would be (Search)-Comprehend-Do, the brackets indicating an element which is often minimal.

Although it seems possible to break down Comprehend-Do tasks into separate subtasks for assessment, there are greater risks to validity in doing this than is the case with Search-Do tasks. The most valid check on the Comprehend element is, in fact, to study how pupils approach the Do element. Any other method of assessing the Comprehend element must be viewed with caution. We surveyed a range of suggested ways of assessing comprehension. However, none of these satisfied the needs of Comprehend-Do reading. One could, when assessing a Comprehend-Do task, set detailed questions such as are asked in interpretation exercises. These might call for detailed comprehension of *all* parts of the text and not just the *relevant* parts. Pupils who scored poorly on these questions might still have understood the text sufficiently well to carry out the Do element successfully. On the other hand, it is quite possible that some pupils might score well on these detailed questions but not be able to carry out what is involved in the Do element. This illustrates the potential limitations of an approach to the formative assessment of Comprehend-Do tasks which concentrates exclusively on the Comprehend element.

Techniques of Item Construction

There are two kinds of Comprehend-Do reading task: the kind of task in which the Do element involves a written response, and the kind of task in which the Do element demands some kind of action other than writing. The first kind appears to present fewer problems for teachers. There are, however, quite severe constraints on the range of Comprehend-Do tasks of the second kind which can be given full rein in the classroom. Nevertheless, the increasing use of worksheets in schools not only increases the importance of Comprehend-Do reading but also gives greater opportunities to observe pupils carrying out both kinds of task in a real situation.

Where a Comprehend-Do task requires an 'action' response, the teacher will often have to fall back on some kind of simulation, with asking questions being the most obvious approach. In these circumstances only a handful of questions directed at the important pieces of information are likely to be necessary. Detailed and elaborate questioning is likely to distort the task.

When real-life Comprehend-Do tasks are presented in schools they will frequently have to be performed out of context. Teachers will have to be sensitive to the demands this puts on the pupils' ability to work from an imagined context. Deficiencies in background knowledge and confusion over sources of information are likely to be highlighted in these circumstances. We were ourselves very surprised at how difficult it was to foresee the amount and kind of extra information which pupils need to possess, or need to be given, when a Comprehend-Do task is undertaken out of context.

Factors to be considered

We provide four diagrams containing questions intended to help teachers when constructing assessment materials for Comprehend-Do reading. In addition, we would suggest that where several very similar texts exist, for example, sets of instructions from different seed packets or sets of instructions from paint labels, it may be useful to construct an assessment unit based on a collection of such texts.

*Diagram 1: Preliminary
Considerations*

Success in Comprehend-Do
reading tasks depends, among
other things, on (a) the amount
of relevant experience which the
pupil has and (b) the context in
which he meets the task.

(a)   EXPERIENCE   AND   (b)   CONTEXT

If the pupil does not have
sufficient previous
experience of this *kind of
task*, can the problem be
overcome through the use of
support materials? (See
Diagrams 2, 3 & 4.)

If the pupil does not have
sufficient experience of the
subject matter to which the
task relates, can the problem
be overcome through
instruction given before the
task is attempted?

If the task cannot be
presented in the real-life
context should pupils:

i) be supplied with an
imaginary context within
which answers are to be
given;

OR

ii) be left to use their own
personal experience and
knowledge to provide a
context for the task?

Diagram 2: Questions about Layout

In the Comprehend element, layout is often a source of difficulty. Pupils can be helped by highlighting. This can be done by (a) inserting graphic aids into the text or (b) questioning.

(a)   GRAPHIC AIDS   OR   (b)   QUESTIONING

Should important parts of the text be highlighted (e.g. underlined) to direct attention to them?	Should the pupils be directed to key pieces of information through questioning?
Should the optimum route through the text be highlighted e.g. by number-coding?	Can the same questions be asked of several texts?

Diagram 3: Questions about Language

In the Comprehend element, the language used in the text is frequently a source of difficulty. Pupils can be helped by (a) glossing or (b) expanding/simplifying the text.

(a)   GLOSSING   OR   (b)   EXPANDING/SIMPLIFYING

Should the difficult words be glossed for the pupils?	Should pupils undertake a preliminary task with an 'expanded' and/or simplified text?

*Diagram 4:   Questions about
the Response Stage*

In the Do element pupils who
have read and understood the
text may experience difficulty in
producing a response in the
required way, that is, (a) an
'action' response (e.g.
assembling a piece of scientific
apparatus) or (b) a written or
oral response (e.g. completing a
form).

(a)   'ACTION' RESPONSES   OR   (b)   WRITTEN OR ORAL
                                                RESPONSES

If the final response involves
activity other than writing, can
pupils be asked to carry out
the necessary *activity*?

If pupils cannot be asked to
carry out the active response,
can it be usefully transformed
into a written or oral
response? ──────────────┐

If the final response is oral or
written:

i) should pupils be asked to
    generate a response and
    produce it orally or
    generate a response and
    write it down?

                    OR

ii) should pupils be asked to
    select their responses
    from a list or table showing
    how others have
    responded?

CHAPTER 6

The Assessment of Personal Response Reading: Novel-Reading (1)

Introduction

In this chapter and the following one we describe our attempts to produce formative assessment materials for use when pupils are reading novels. Reading novels falls within our Comprehend-Personal Response category of reading tasks. When novels are read in English courses, readers are expected to do more than simply 'understand the story': they are expected to respond to and interpret the contents of the novel through reflecting on their own experiences and relating these to the events, situations and themes presented by the author. Pupils may also be asked to offer an aesthetic judgment on the text. This view of the nature of Comprehend-Personal Response reading clearly implies that it would be quite inappropriate to produce assessment materials where pupils' responses would be judged merely on a right/wrong basis.

For many teachers the essence of mature novel-reading lies in the ability to respond to ideas and images on the basis of personal experience and aesthetic sensibility. If such responses are to be encouraged then assessment procedures based solely on the comprehension model will not be adequate. It is difficult to argue, however, that assessment of the comprehension element in novel-reading is wholly inappropriate. When discussing novels with pupils, teachers assume some degree of shared understanding of aspects such as character, motivation and development of the plot.

Without this understanding, a pupil is unlikely to be able to communicate a personal response to the teacher and the teacher's comments on the text are likely to be puzzling to the pupil. We discuss this further in Chapters 8 and 9.

In thinking about appropriate assessment techniques we had also to bear in mind that teachers stress that novels are to be read principally for enjoyment. Therefore, any procedure likely to detract from pupils' enjoyment had to be avoided if possible. On the other hand, it is somewhat perverse to argue that enjoying a novel is not somehow bound up with 'understanding' it. In the teaching of English, for example, there is an underlying assumption that enjoyment of a novel is likely to be increased if the reader's ability to analyse and evaluate the material is developed. If this is true, it should be possible to construct assessment procedures which enhance the reader's enjoyment.

In devising techniques for the formative assessment of novel reading, we had to consider not simply *whether* a novel had been understood but also *how* it had been understood. The assessment material would have to allow pupils to demonstrate the nature and content of their responses. It should help to reveal factors which might be constraining these responses. For example, one constraining factor which our materials did, in fact, reveal was that some pupils had little grasp of the technical terms used in character description. The research team remains convinced that, as a means of eliciting and examining such responses, there is no real substitute for discussion with individual pupils or groups of pupils. The assessment materials we constructed were an attempt to create a basis for such discussion. We hoped that they would be especially useful in eliciting responses from reticent pupils and from those who have difficulty in expressing themselves.

Seeking a Formative Approach

We began our investigations into Comprehend-Personal Response reading by carrying out a preliminary study of what might be involved in the reading of one particular novel. The novel used was *The Pit* (Maddock, 1969) from the Macmillan Topliner series, a novel which is widely used in schools. We devised assessment units which we thought might illuminate how pupils coped with this text.

In reading a novel, readers have to use what the author says in the text to reconstruct for themselves the characters, situations and events that make up the story. To do this they need to call upon their own knowledge and background experience. It follows that one reader's reconstruction may vary significantly from that of another. Thus the Personal Response element is not easily separated from the Comprehension element. In planning for formative assessment of novel-reading it did not seem appropriate, therefore, to assume that there would be one 'correct' or 'definitive' reading and to look for evidence that this reading had been achieved. It seemed much more appropriate to try to find out what *kind* of imaginative reconstruction had taken place. Our efforts were directed, then, at producing some kind of activity which might (a) demonstrate that pupils were actively engaged in some kind of reconstruction even if they found this difficult to express, and (b) provoke responses which the teacher could use in discussion.

With this particular text we introduced three units which we hoped would illuminate pupils' capacity for this kind of imaginative reconstruction. In the first we looked at pupils' imaginative reconstructions of the physical environment. We then provided a unit to try to gather information about pupils' impressions of characters and the relationships between them. Finally, we tried to get some insights into how pupils understood and retained the sequence of events in the novel. In the remainder of this chapter we report on school trials using these units.

Imaginative Reconstruction of the Physical Environment

In 'The Pit' the physical environment has virtually the status of a theme. Butch, the hero, repeatedly asserts the superiority of country over town, and even of country people over town people. There is considerable detail about Barnton (where Butch lives) and its immediate surroundings. The first unit in the collection of assessment materials was based, therefore, on a picture map of the area in which the story takes place. On the map, important places in the story were marked with letters and a short set of questions was prepared. To answer each question pupils had to select the appropriate letter.

The first question we asked was 'Which letter marks the church in Grimthorpe?' We were not, in fact, interested in Grimthorpe church itself but used the church to check whether readers had distinguished between two important places mentioned in the story, Grimthorpe and Barnton. Grimthorpe is an industrial town on the plain halfway to the sea. Barnton, on the other hand, is a small rural town further inland on the edge of the moors. On the map Grimthorpe was shown with several industrial chimneys and a pit-head. To find formative information we looked beyond the answers pupils gave and took note of how they justified these answers.

The Findings

1. *Making use of information from the text*

In the justifications given for answers to the first question we looked for evidence that the industrial image of Grimthorpe had been grasped.

Here are three of the justifications offered by pupils who responded with the correct answer, (C), to this question.

Which letter marks the church in Grimthorpe?

'Grimthorpe is the industrial town and C looks like a church.'

'Grimthorpe is supposed to be an industrial town.'

'Grimthorpe was where all the men from the other place had to go for their work – and it was a big industrial city – and it is the biggest church of the two.'

These three pupils based their justifications on the fact that Grimthorpe was the industrial town. They had therefore relied on information from the text in making their responses.

2. *Relying too much on information from sources other than the
   text*

Pupils who got Question 1 wrong tended to do so because they did
not use the information in the text to help them to answer the
question. (This does not necessarily mean that they did not have
the information.) For example, one pupil who produced the
'wrong' answer explained that he just 'looked for a church and a
steeple.' In justifying his answer he relied on information provided
in the question and in the map rather than on information from the
novel itself.

With almost every question we were able to distinguish between
pupils who used information from the novel to produce and justify
their answers and pupils who relied almost exclusively on
information from the question, the map or from their own
experience. We provide a further illustration with reference to
Question 6: 'Which letter marks the place where Butch and Skiff
had a fight after school?' Two fields are marked on the map. The
field near the school is marked with the letter M while another
field, some considerable distance from the school, is marked with
the letter O. Here are the justifications of two pupils, both of
whom got the right answer (M).

---

*Which letter marks the place where Butch and Skiff had
a fight after school?*

'You wouldn't want to walk to O for a fight.'

'The boys opened the gate in the Highfield Road. It
was round the corner from Long Lane. Butch was
hiding behind the hedge.'

The first pupil's justification is sensible (perhaps even based on
actual experience) but makes no reference at all to what is actually
stated in the novel. On the other hand, the second pupil recollects
in some detail the relevant part of the text. Notice the importance
of probing beyond answers to find out how pupils are actually
thinking. The justifications pupils give for their answers should be

a major focus of attention in formative assessment.

When justifying their answers, pupils varied substantially in the weighting they gave to information from the novel, from the map and from everyday experience. Mature novel-reading involves striking some kind of balance between the use of novel-based and experience-based inferences in arriving at interpretations and evaluations. The reader who fails to make use of his or her own experience will not fully engage with the text and will not make the personal response essential for novel reading. On the other hand, the reader who allows his own experience to overwhelm the text will not find novel reading enriching and illuminating in the way teachers hope it should be. When answering questions, a pupil's tendency to depend on sources of information other than the novel itself may be of considerable diagnostic value. It is unlikely to be noticed, however, if pupils are specifically directed to use information from the novel in offering justifications for answers. When instructions are altered in this way, we cease to observe the pupils' *spontaneous* strategy. Such directions would be useful, however, where initial questioning has revealed a tendency to ignore the content of the novel.

3.   *Associating the physical environment with actions of characters*

Pupils rarely used explicit geographical references in their reasoning without tying this to the actions of characters in the novel. One reason why some pupils found it difficult to identify Grimthorpe may have been that it is *not* the centre of any of the activities of the main characters. In explaining how they identified Widow Baxter's house, several pupils described it as being 'at the end of Long Lane (geographical) and Butch had to pass it to get to the farm (action).' This finding – that pupils thought about places in the novel in terms of actions rather than in purely geographical terms – may have theoretical and practical implications. For some pupils, producing an imaginative reconstruction of the environment may depend on the extent to which significant actions in the story are identifiable with particular locations. If the environment is seen simply as a backdrop to events its significance may go unrecognised.

In concluding this section we would point out that, although the map was carefully prepared, it is not essential in this kind of work that it be absolutely accurate. Inaccuracies inevitably occur. The reactions these provoke may give insight into the extent of pupils' memory for detail. In one class we were able to collect pupils' own comments on the map. Five of them criticised the placing of the pubs – 'The pubs are too close . . . in competition'! Several others pointed out that Grimthorpe should be bigger. The very fact that these pupils criticised the map showed that they had some internal reconstruction of the setting for the story.

This unit was successful in that it provided a means of checking whether or not pupils had picked up information about the physical background to the novel.

Characters and the Relationships Between Them

English teachers argue that through novel-reading pupils gain an insight into how people behave in everyday life. Many attempts have been made to get readers to express their ideas about the characters in a novel and the relationships between them. Techniques which have been used by psychologists to investigate how people perceive human personality characteristics, such as Repertory Grid Tests and the Semantic Differential, have been adapted to study readers' responses to characters in novels or short stories. These psychological techniques, however, seemed to us too formal and forbidding to be useful for the pupils we were working with.

What we needed was a simple technique which would allow pupils to express their ideas about the characters in the novel. Instead of asking pupils to produce descriptions of characters, our unit asked them to select characters to fit given descriptions. Each item in the assessment unit consisted of a question or a statement and an accompanying table showing the names of the principal characters. In responding to each item, the pupil had to draw a line round the name of each of the characters he or she selected. For example, the first item in this assessment unit asked pupils to indicate people in the story whom Butch liked. Since the novel is written exclusively from Butch's point of view this was not a difficult item. Overleaf we show how one pupil responded to this item.

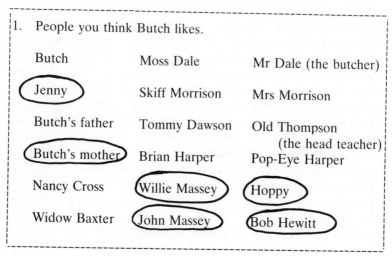

Figure 10:   One Pupil's Response to Item 1 in the 'Pit People' Unit

We would argue that this task is much less demanding and much less abstract than asking pupils to provide descriptions of nominated characters. Furthermore, it encourages pupils to think about the similarities and differences among characters and this can be particularly helpful. The assessment items appear simple but a carefully prepared collection of them can be quite powerful in revealing how pupils think about characters. Here we summarise our main findings.

The Findings

Evidence from classroom trials with this assessment unit suggests that it might be used in several ways.

1. *The unit might be used to support pupils' thinking about the characters.*

Pupils may have formed quite definite impressions about the characters in a novel but may not be able to put these impressions into words. After all, even adults sometimes find it difficult to offer considered descriptions of friends and acquaintances. The technique supports pupils in two ways. Firstly, in comparison with writing a character description, this task gives readers a simple way of recording their impressions. Secondly, it offers them possible ideas and vocabulary to consider in attempting to formulate these impressions. This support function is similar to that offered by other techniques used in the project; e.g. the use of expanded versions of forms (Chapter 5) or of systematic questioning to aid understanding of short stories (Chapter 8).

Once pupils have worked through a unit of this kind, they can gather together information about a particular character by looking through the tables they have completed. For example, a pupil might have indicated in his responses to different tables that Butch was violent, admired people who worked on the land, disliked his father but liked his mother and sister, was honest for the most part and was a strong character. As suggested by several teachers, this information can be abstracted from the tables and written up as a simple character description.

2. *The unit might be used to check on pupils' understanding of terms used to describe characters*

As in all our work we asked pupils to justify the selections they made. The explanations pupils gave for their decisions indicated what *they had understood* by the terms used in character description. When we asked pupils to indicate 'People who are weak or feeble' some pupils interpreted this in terms of personality while others responded in terms of physical characteristics. Thus, Widow Baxter was 'weak' 'because she was old'. In the next item we asked pupils to indicate 'People who have a strong personality'. Some pupils continued to think in terms of physical strength. Here is how one pupil explained her selection of characters to fit the description, 'People who hide their feelings'.

Jenny	She is usually quiet.
Butch's mother	She is just the same as Jenny.
Nancy Cross	When she comes in the house she usually just peeps in the door: she doesn't really come in.
Widow Baxter	She's stuck up in her house: she doesn't seem to come out.

For this pupil, 'hiding one's feelings' is almost a matter of 'hiding oneself'.

Judicious preparation of a collection of items containing adjectives or phrases similar in meaning may help the teacher to gather evidence about whether fine but important distinctions have been recognised. Used like this, the technique is intended not so much to support character description but rather to find out the pupil's understanding of terms commonly used in character descriptions. Thus, by comparing the ways in which pupils made selections from the table of characters accompanying two of our statements, we found that most pupils distinguished between 'people Butch likes' and 'people Butch admires or looks up to'.

3.   *The unit might be used to reveal something of how pupils perceive interpersonal attitudes and relationships*

The simplest kind of item required pupils to give *their own impressions of the characters*. Did the pupils think that Butch was violent? Did they think that Widow Baxter had a strong personality? Other items in the unit demanded more than this. These items asked pupils to empathise with the characters to the extent that they could identify *one character's impression of other characters*. For example, pupils were asked to draw lines round the names of characters they thought Butch looked up to or admired. This kind of item is a good deal more complex. Bruce & Newman (1978) have shown how readers need to think at this level if even quite simple stories are to be understood. In many children's stories, the actions of a character make sense only if it is understood that he or she has perceived, and made allowance for, the 'plan' decided upon by another character. It is by this kind of thinking that the third little pig outsmarts the Big Bad Wolf!

Our data suggest that many pupils find some difficulty in discussing one character's attitude towards another. For example, most pupils decided that Butch liked Jenny. Some pupils could provide evidence to support their contention: 'When his Dad hit Jenny, Butch went mad.' Others, however, could only offer statements like 'Jenny is his sister. She is kind to him.' Neither of these sentences contains clear evidence that Butch likes Jenny. Yet it is this kind of 'second level' thinking about how one character relates to another that is necessary for more advanced criticism of novels.

Two further points are worth noting briefly. Firstly, character tables can be a useful stimulus to group activity. Groups of pupils can argue out which characters they will select in a particular item. Alternatively, groups can discuss items for which they have already made their own individual selections. Secondly, pupils themselves can be asked to produce items. These items may reflect something of their approach to characters in novels.

Although literary criticism is full of analyses of characters and disputes about the validity of characters, little has been written about how pupils develop an understanding of characters and the relationships between them. If, as many English teachers would claim, such understanding built up within the artificial world of the novel helps pupils to think about similar problems in the real world, then we need to find out much more about its development.

Following the Plot

Reading a novel is a substantial intellectual feat. Besides the re-creative effort discussed in the previous sections, the reader has to maintain a grasp of plot and subplot over a considerable period of time. Failure to do this reduces the novel to a series of incidents and makes it much less interesting and meaningful as a consequence. Thus, while we may share, at least in some degree, E.M. Forster's attitude to the story in a novel – 'Yes – oh dear, yes – the novel tells a story' – we would argue that following the story is an important and fundamental part of the novel-reading process. (We are aware that not all novels have recognisable plots, but these are usually reserved for pupils pursuing more advanced courses in literature.) We found no published research relating to how readers cope with plots and subplots in novels.

We wanted to devise a means of finding out *if* and *how* a reader was 'storing' the important events in a novel. By an 'important' event we mean one which makes a difference to the story; i.e. it changes the situation or produces certain consequences. One way to do this would be to ask pupils to retell the story or part of it, but this has several disadvantages. In the first place, pupils who have followed and remembered the events in the novel may not be able to provide a fluent oral account of the plot. Recall is a very demanding way of measuring retention. Secondly, there is a tendency for pupils to offer a much abbreviated version of a story when they know that the listener has also read it.

Our approach was to present brief descriptions of events or situations from the novel in groups of three. One of the three events was 'important' in the limited sense that it did 'make a difference' to the story. This we will call the 'central' event.

Of the other two, one description was of an incident or situation which preceded the central one and the other referred to an incident or situation which followed it. The reader was simply asked to put the three events in the order in which they happened in the novel. (Unlike our 'Pit People' unit, the items in this unit did have right answers.) Notice that the pupils had only one chance in six of arriving at the right answer by random guessing. Usually, multiple choice questions offer a one-in-four chance.

The Findings

To cope with the items in this unit pupils had to recognise the incidents in the novel, and by a process of recall or reasoning, indicate the sequence in which they happened. When we considered the results of school trials in terms of the number of items correctly sequenced we found that some pupils were noticeably weak on this unit. Such pupils often remarked that they could not remember particular incidents.

Some of the items proved to be considerably more difficult than others. A few items had been deliberately constructed to check on one anticipated source of difficulty. In these the three events to be sequenced were drawn from quite different subplots in the novel and were, therefore, not *directly* related to each other. These items, as predicted, turned out to be quite difficult. Even pupils who got them right could not really justify their answers.

There were other items, however, where the degree of difficulty surprised us. Once again it was the pupils' explanations for their answers which offered some insight into the kind of factors which might make one item more difficult than another. We use one particularly difficult item, Item B, to illustrate this. The item is reproduced opposite with the correct sequence written in underneath.

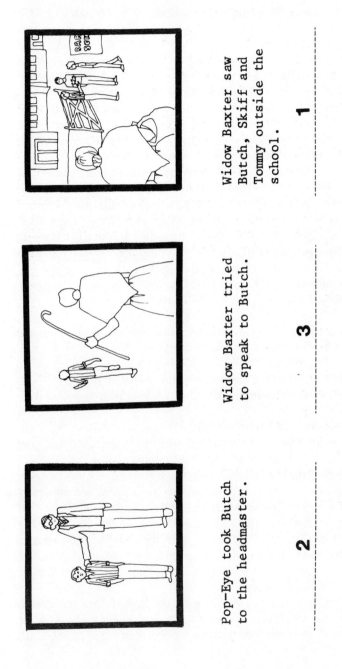

Figure 11: Item B in the 'Pit Story' unit

We can justify this sequence as follows. When Butch met Skiff and Tommy outside school they gave him two of the stolen biscuits. The next day, Butch produced one of these in class and Pop-Eye spotted it. He took Butch to the headmaster. When Widow Baxter later heard that Butch had been accused of the theft she tried to speak to him but he kept running away.

To see where the difficulty lies in this item we need to distinguish between two time sequences: the time sequence of the events in the novel as they happen, and the time sequence of the events as they are reported by the author. The fact that Widow Baxter saw Butch, Skiff and Tommy outside the school at the time of the theft is only *revealed* after Pop-Eye took Butch to the headmaster, although it did in fact *occur* before this. The Widow is trying to tell Butch that she saw all three boys outside the school. The author has, therefore, used a kind of flashback device to sustain the excitement of his plot. In doing this, however, he has introduced a potential source of difficulty.

Some pupils explicitly mentioned the problem and, at the same time, showed that they had no difficulty in coping with it:

'Later in the story she owned up that she'd seen them outside school, so I thought it must have come first.'

'Because, when the police questioned Widow Baxter she said she had seen Tommy, Skiff and Butch outside the school.'

Awareness of the problem did not always result in the right answer being given, as can be seen by the responses and explanations reproduced in Figure 12 opposite.

The first of these pupils has failed to reason out the full answer. It is clear that her explanation contains the information necessary to produce the correct sequence. ('She had seen them that night . . .') Yet she fails to recognise that the logic of her explanations demands that she reverse the order of the first two incidents. On the other hand, the second pupil distorts the content of the novel to justify his answer: 'Later that day Widow Baxter was out for messages, etc.'

Quite early in the development of the material we recognised the importance of trying to understand what makes an item of this kind difficult. We introduced items which asked pupils to sequence

Events and Placings

Reasons for Placings

First Pupil   Second Pupil

(Placed first,
correct placing second)

"Because he saw
Butch had bis-
cuits and thought
Butch had stolen
them."

"Pop-Eye thought he
had stolen and he
was taken right to
the headmaster. He
told him he didn't
steal but no one
would believe him."

Pop-Eye took Butch
to the headmaster.

(Placed second,
correct placing first)

"She had seen them
that night and
she'd seen who
was to blame, who
had broken into
the school."

"Later that day
Widow Baxter was
out for messages
and she saw Butch,
Skiff and Tommy
outside the school."

Widow Baxter saw
Butch, Skiff and
Tommy outside the
school.

(Placed third,
correct placing third)

"She wanted to
speak to him
about the breaking
in that night and
she tried to tell
the police what
she had seen."

"Widow Baxter tried
to speak to Butch
about what had
happened - he was
supposed to have
been stealing the
biscuit."

Widow Baxter tried
to speak to Butch.

Figure 12: Pupils' reasons for sequences offered for Item B

events drawn from different subplots in the novel. Such items did appear to be more difficult than items constructed using events drawn from the same subplot. Other factors, however, seemed to be affecting the difficulty level of items. For example, events used to build an item can be referred to directly or more obliquely by describing an associated happening. We suspect that items using oblique references to events may be more difficult. A study of what makes some items more difficult than others may be a way of exploring how readers represent and store events when reading stories.

Conclusions

In this chapter we have described three different techniques which might be used to construct materials for the formative assessment of novel-reading. In each case the most useful information about pupils' reading came not from the answers themselves but from the explanations pupils offered for their answers. The techniques used to investigate pupils' understanding of characters and to study their ability to follow and reason about the plot are potentially powerful and flexible. For example, it would be possible for teachers to construct items to study pupils' recognition of quite specific qualities in a particular character in a novel and to use the same technique to check on an individual pupil's grasp of the more general terms used in character description.

Note

The techniques discussed in this chapter were devised as a result of a close study of one sample novel. Difficulties in novel-reading cannot be adequately explored on the basis of work done with only one, fairly straightforward novel. We needed to study a more advanced novel not only to check whether the techniques could be usefully applied to it but also to consider how the range of techniques might be extended. In the next chapter we describe our work on assessing the reading of a more advanced novel.

CHAPTER 7

The Assessment of Personal Response Reading: Novel-Reading (2)

Introduction

The techniques and materials described in the previous chapter were not the only ones used with 'The Pit'. The other materials we had prepared proved unsatisfactory in one way or another. When we moved on to consider a second sample novel, therefore, we were concerned not simply to find out whether the three techniques already described could be applied to another similar text but also to see whether we could provide alternative approaches to replace the weaker material. Even more important, however, was the conviction that assessment techniques found useful with one text should not be applied to another without first appraising how appropriate they are to the new text and to the purpose pupils have for reading it. Thus, when we turned to a second sample novel we had *three* questions in mind.

1. Three techniques had produced useful assessment units for pupils working with 'The Pit'. Could we use these techniques to produce practical and worthwhile units for use with a more advanced novel?

2. Could we extend the range of techniques to cope with important aspects of the new novel which were not present in 'The Pit'?

3. Some of the assessment units constructed for use with 'The Pit' were found to be less than satisfactory in school trials. Could we improve the techniques we had used to construct these units?

The second novel we worked on was *Pennington's Seventeenth Summer* (Peyton, 1970). This was a more sophisticated novel than 'The Pit' and demanded more of the reader.

Applying Existing Techniques

We found it appropriate to construct 'Pennington' units similar to the three 'Pit' units described in the previous chapter. We therefore prepared units designed (a) to assess pupils' ability to produce an imaginative reconstruction of the physical environment; (b) to assess pupils' impressions of characters and of the relationships between them; and (c) to assess the extent to which pupils were able to follow the plot. Although we were unable to acquire as much data as we did for the 'Pit' units, the results we obtained supported our earlier findings. For example, we again found pupils who had difficulty in sequencing events from the novel. The results suggested that these techniques can provide useful formative information even with a more sophisticated novel.

Both the character and plot assessment units were so designed that, if desired, they could be used at intervals during the reading of a novel. By the end of the project several teachers had used them in this way. They reported that this use of the character unit was particularly profitable. Pupils could see how and if their own view of characters changed as they read the novel. Using items from the plot unit at appropriate intervals while reading the novel helped to remind pupils of previous events and enabled teachers to check that important connections had been made. This informal use of the material may be more relevant to the ongoing handling of a novel in the classroom context.

Developing New Techniques

1. *The question of realism*

'Pennington's Seventeenth Summer' differs from 'The Pit' in that the author introduces several passages of sustained detailed description in an attempt to build up the boating and musical background against which the events of the novel are set. Consequently, a good deal of unfamiliar vocabulary is introduced. 'Halyards' and 'bowlines' are mentioned and Pennington has to cope with an 'andante capriccioso', which he performs at 'a very ambitious tempo without loss of clarity'! If the presentation of the novel to inexperienced or unskilful readers is seen purely as requiring simplification of the text, then teachers would presumably encourage the 'skipping' of such passages. On the other hand it may be felt that such passages are of considerable importance and contribute to some of the cumulative though diffuse effects which the novel exerts on the reader. If the second position is accepted, then 'Pennington' demands a form of reading which is distinctive of 'realistic' fiction.

We looked for a simple way of acquiring evidence that the descriptions used to build up the boating and musical background in 'Pennington' did have some effect upon pupils. We hypothesised that these descriptions would have an effect on pupils' recognition vocabularies, i.e. we hypothesised that through reading 'Pennington' pupils would come to acquire boating or musical connotations for words met in the novel. How could we test this hypothesis?

THE 'BOATS AND MUSIC' UNIT

When the boating and musical terms were listed it was found that there was a high proportion of polysemous words, i.e. words which have more than one meaning. For example, among the music words we find 'tenth', 'scale', 'key' and 'movement', and among the boating words we find 'sheet', 'spit', 'trim' and 'craft'. In each case the word is used in the novel in a specialised sense. Some interesting, though hardly definitive, research has been done on how readers cope with polysemous words. A distinction is made between the very familiar, *primary* meaning of a polysemous word and its less familiar, less common or specialised *secondary* meaning. Hogoboam & Perfetti (1975) produced evidence which suggested that when 'reading a passage', the secondary sense of a word is considered only if the primary meaning does not fit the context. This work was conducted with adults. Mason, Knisely & Kendall (1979), working with children aged ten to twelve, found that primary meanings were often preferred even when the word was placed in a sentence which clearly demanded the secondary meaning. The primary meaning has a high potency which has to be overcome by the context. This is particularly the case with children of lower reading ability.

Normally, pupils will give the primary meaning of words unless the context supports a secondary one. Even where the context is supportive of the secondary meaning, they will still demonstrate a strong tendency to offer the primary meaning. In 'Pennington's Seventeenth Summer', the reader encounters the secondary meanings of words in a strong context. (Research to date has used single sentences to provide the context.) We hypothesised that if the boating and musical background to the novel had an impact on the reader, then this might show in an increased sensitivity to secondary and specialised meanings.

Our purposes would not be served by introducing a straightforward vocabulary test. Adults have been happily reading Hornblower novels for years without being able to explain exactly what is meant by 'luffing' or 'mizzen-tops' and so on. Yet they would be able to recognise these as nautical terms. We therefore did not want to test whether the reader could produce a definition of 'freeboard' or even recognise a drawing of a halyard if he saw it. This would be too demanding a task, requiring an approach to novel-reading akin to the technique used for interpretation exercises. An alternative approach had to be found.

A possible solution was to adapt the method proposed by Anderson & Freebody (1979) as a technique to be used generally for the assessment of vocabulary. The child is presented with a list of words and asked to indicate which words he 'knows'. So that a correction can be made for guessing, a proportion of nonsense words is introduced into the list. The authors point out that this technique is only suitable for checking that the pupil knows one meaning of the word. 'It is apparent that the yes/no format is not suitable for distinguishing which of the meanings of a word are unknown. When that is the goal, some other method of assessment is required' (p.32).

The approach we developed is a modification of Anderson & Freebody's. We presented the pupils with a list of words taken from 'Pennington's Seventeenth Summer'. Of the forty-five words in the list fifteen were boating/sailing terms, fifteen were music terms and fifteen were other words. Some of the words (e.g. 'capriccioso') were specialist terms, while others were reasonably common words with a secondary, specialised meaning in boating or musical contexts (e.g. 'craft'). We presented these randomly in a list (see Figure 13) and asked the pupils to indicate the boating terms. They were then asked to do the same with the musical terms. The pupils were therefore *given* the general semantic categories into which the words had to be placed. They were not asked to give precise definitions. This seemed to us to approximate quite closely to the level of meaning required in handling these words in a novel. The task is comparatively unthreatening and it takes only a short time to administer. At no point during the reading of the novel was there an attempt to teach the meaning of these terms. Any explicit teaching of these vocabularies would run counter to our approach and indeed invalidate it.

Pupils were asked to attempt the task *before* they read the novel and to do it again *after* they had read it. The two performances were then compared. A control group of comparable pupils was used to give a basis for comparison.

The findings

Our hypothesis was that after reading the novel, pupils would 'recognise' more words on the list as being boating and music terms than they had before reading it. To achieve this they would have to recognise some words they had never met before reading the novel, and overcome a tendency to consider only the primary meaning of some of the other words on the list.

We undertook two studies. We did not have high expectations of success in this experiment. Indeed, on the first pilot run with the materials, it was almost as an afterthought that we used a control class. This class did not read the novel but worked through the assessment unit at the same times as did the experimental class. In our second study we made some changes to the materials and to the way in which they were used. We do not claim, however, to

Boats and Music

Here are some words. Write the letter **B** in the box beside each word that would be used in writing about boats or sailing. Write the letter **M** in the box beside each word that would be used in writing about music. Leave all the other boxes empty.

Here are four examples which are done for you:

solid . . . . ☐
mast . . . . Ⓑ
tune . . . . Ⓜ
scenery . . . . ☐

Now do the same with these:–

1. anchor . . . . . ☐	16. movement . ☐	31. bowline . . . . ☐
2. malice . . . . . ☐	17. impending . ☐	32. craft . . . . ☐
3. spit . . . . ☐	18. saloon . . . . . ☐	33. cellulose . . . ☐
4. bonkers . . . . ☐	19. chord . . . . . . ☐	34. polonaise . . ☐
5. bulwarks . . . ☐	20. blues . . . . . . ☐	35. tiller . . . . . . ☐
6. octave . . . . . ☐	21. halyard . . . . ☐	36. trim . . . . ☐
7. outright . . . . ☐	22. sheet . . . . . . ☐	37. companion ☐
8. capriccioso ☐	23. scarpered . . ☐	38. key . . . . ☐
9. stern . . . . . . ☐	24. guitar . . . . . ☐	39. accompany ☐
10. pressure . . . ☐	25. respray . . . . ☐	40. dissolvent . . ☐
11. tenth . . . . . . ☐	26. integrity . . . ☐	41. soul . . . . ☐
12. moquette . . ☐	27. andante . . . . ☐	42. neon . . . . . . ☐
13. smack . . . . . ☐	28. midriff . . . . . ☐	43. scale . . . . . . ☐
14. folk . . . . ☐	29. elation . . . . . ☐	44. jib . . . . ☐
15. dinghy . . . . . ☐	30. dynamic . . . ☐	45. harmonica . ☐

Figure 13:   Sample sheet from 'Boats and Music' Unit (Sheet BMI)

have conducted a rigorous experiment. We had neither the time nor the resources to do so.

In both studies the data analyses (based on signal detection theory) uncovered a trend consistent with our hypothesis. After they had read the novel, pupils did recognise more boating and music words. This attained statistical significance in the case of our second study. The pupils in the control group showed no such improvement. (Unfortunately, each study was marred by the fact that the control group scored higher on the pre-test than did the experimental group who went on to read the novel.)

This significant difference was achieved despite the fact that some words were recognised as boating or music words on the first testing by 100% of the pupils. Clearly, a quite dramatic improvement had to be made on the remaining words if a statistically significant gain was to be recorded overall. That such an improvement was made in certain cases can be seen from some examples quoted below.

Table 1: **Words whose rate of recognition showed dramatic increase in the experimental group**

| | Experimental Group | |
	1st 'Test'	*2nd 'Test'*
Music		
tenth	40.7%	66.7%
polonaise	11.0%	41.0%
Boats		
spit	22.2%	48.1%
smack	14.8%	63.0%
halyard	55.5%	81.5%

All of the distractor words functioned successfully, some of them with spectacular success. 'Moquette' clearly looks like a musical word. It was selected as such by 59% (first testing) and 70% (second testing) of the experimental group and by 46% (first testing) and 50% (second testing) of the control group. Similarly, reading the novel, if anything, confirmed the experimental group in their belief that 'midriff' is a nautical term (81% and 89%): the control group were similarly distracted (71% and 89%)!

It is important at this stage to bear in mind the principal aims of the project. We were concerned to investigate assessment techniques which classroom teachers might adapt for use with their own texts and in their own classrooms. It would have been surprising (and gratifying) if, in this kind of research, the data had produced a clear-cut, statistically acceptable result. Nonetheless, the investigation did suggest that useful information and perhaps a useful basis for class or group discussion can be found by adopting this approach. It has always been assumed that reading novels has an impact on vocabulary development but there has been little experimental evidence to support this assumption. Our approach *might* be useful in the search for such evidence. We leave it to others to design and carry out the more rigorous experimentation which is needed to produce evidence that reading novels does have a significant impact on vocabulary.

2. *Understanding conflict*

Steinberg & Bruce (1980) suggest that there are significant differences between novels in terms of the levels of conflict described. They argue that conflict is an essential feature of any story or novel. At the simplest level, conflict is essentially *environmental conflict*; i.e. the character or characters will find their goals frustrated by factors such as shipwreck, flood, etc. At a 'higher' level there is straightforward *conflict between characters*. Thus, in 'Pennington's Seventeenth Summer', we have a confrontation between Pennington and 'Soggy' Marsh over whether Pennington should have his hair cut. The third type of conflict is *internal conflict*. In 'The Pit' Butch is torn between conforming to the rule against carrying tales to authority and having to take the blame for a crime committed by Skiff. Though there is undoubtedly a degree of internal conflict built into 'The Pit', it is limited. 'Pennington's Seventeenth Summer', on the other hand, is studded with the development and resolution of internal conflict. We are allowed to see conflict not just in the mind of Pennington, but in the thinking of his teachers, his friends and other characters.

None of the techniques we devised for use with 'The Pit' probed readers' perceptions of such conflict situations. For 'Pennington's Seventeenth Summer' we constructed a 'Whose Problem?' unit which required pupils to identify problems. They had to read a description of an internal conflict in 'Pennington's Seventeenth Summer', recognise the character who had to resolve this conflict, and select the solution in a matching task.

THE 'WHOSE PROBLEM?' UNIT

We used a straightforward matching exercise. On one card problems were described. Each description was in two parts, each pair describing one element in the conflict. For each 'problem' the reader had to select an answer card which gave the solution to the conflict as reported in the novel. For example, one of the items presented the reader with the following conflict situation or problem:

1. 'If he doesn't take part we are going to lose.'

2. 'But he has been banned from doing this.'

3. ？ (Solution)

This referred to Mr Matthews' dilemma about whether he should enter Pennington in the crucial race in the swimming gala despite the fact that he had been explicitly banned from participating in sport. The reader had to select the solution from a set of 10 cards. In this case, the appropriate card was:

'I'll risk it and tell him to do it.'

To create this kind of item the descriptions had to be stripped of most of their specific referents. It was felt that this might prove too difficult for some pupils, and so an alternative format was produced where stronger cues were introduced into the problem descriptions (but not the solution cards). Thus, for the same question, the strong-cued version was as follows:

1. 'If Pennington doesn't take part Beehive is going to lose.'

2. 'But Pennington's been banned from games.'

3. ？ (Solution)

The strong cueing should make the task easier. Because the solution cards were *identical* in both formats, it was a simple matter to substitute the strong-cued version if a pupil was having difficulty. The pupil would still be able to follow and participate in any discussion. In later trials we introduced an extended answer sheet which asked pupils to enter the name of the character experiencing the conflict and to give one or two details to show that they had, in fact, identified the conflict in question.

The findings

What is involved in tackling this task? The reader has to identify the person whose conflict is being described. He has then to find the card which best represents the way in which that person solved the problem in the novel. In doing so he has to identify to whom the terms 'he', 'we', 'this', 'I', 'it', etc. refer, using his knowledge of the story and characters. There are considerable possibilities for discussion, not least because of the different types of solution: compromise, willingness to take risks, perseverance.

From our observations of pupils working with and without the extended answer sheet we noted the following points:

1. Some pupils thought that the statements represented what people said rather than what they were thinking. This difficulty might be avoided if the statements were presented using cartoon conventions. 'Thoughts' could then be inserted in bubbles connected to blank heads by a string of circles. We suspect that the vast majority of pupils would be familiar with this convention.

2. Pupils performed well on the matching task but sometimes the success was due to their manipulation of the material rather than their understanding of the novel. For example, some pupils worked out the answers to several items but then selected the answers to the remainder largely by the process of elimination. Once again we found instances where pupils tackled the assessment task without relating it to the text which had been read. In almost every study we undertook we found some pupils who responded in this way.

3. Pupils were quite good at identifying the relevant incidents in the novel and in describing the immediate circumstances in which the events took place. The materials themselves, however, do not necessarily show that the pupils were also aware of the conflict in the situation. It is a defect of the approach that it focuses the pupils' attention on finding the solution rather than on the conflict itself.

While we remain convinced that the perception and understanding of conflict, particularly internal conflict, is an important element in novel-reading, our own approach is not entirely satisfactory.

Revising Unsatisfactory Techniques

1. *Anticipations*

In the assessment materials for 'The Pit' we included a 'Predictions' exercise which was to be completed *after* the novel had been read. This involved predicting what was going to happen to Butch in the future. An extract is given in Figure 14 overleaf.

In retrospect, this seemed a rather unsatisfactory exercise because, as several teachers suggested, it was too divorced from the actual reading of the novel to yield formative information. For 'Pennington's Seventeenth Summer' we adopted a different approach.

THE 'WHAT'S GOING TO HAPPEN?' UNIT
Some current models of the reading process suggest that anticipation and prediction are key features of fluent reading. They are important controlling forces. We therefore wanted an exercise which would induce pupils to produce anticipations *during* the reading of the novel. For 'Pennington's Seventeenth Summer' we produced an anticipation exercise to be tackled *while* the novel was being read. The anticipation material was designed to probe aspects of novel-reading not tapped by the previous prediction exercise we prepared for use with 'The Pit'. The materials are reproduced on page 111 (Figure 15).

Suppose Butch is a real person and the story of 'The Pit' really happened. Here are some things that might happen in his life after 'The Pit'. Imagine that Butch begins to work harder at school and that his teachers understand him a lot better. Some of the things are *likely* to happen: put a tick (√) at these. Some are *unlikely* to happen: put a cross (×) at these. With some of them it is very hard to decide whether they would happen or not: put a circle (○) against these.

...... Butch's homework gets better.
...... Butch's homework gets worse.
...... Butch still doesn't work hard at homework.
...... Butch starts to behave very badly in class.
...... Butch often stays away from school.
...... Butch becomes much happier at school.
...... Butch shows the teachers he can read well.

Figure 14: Extract from 'Predictions' unit used with 'The Pit'

The basic assessment unit (Sheet A) consisted of a list of sentences, each of which described a possible development in the novel. After they had read a substantial part of the novel, pupils were asked to indicate which of these developments they thought were likely to happen and which they thought were unlikely to happen. They did this by simply writing 'Yes' or 'No'. 'Can't say' was recorded by writing a question mark. The identical list of sentences was presented on two later occasions in slightly different formats (Sheets B & C) so that anticipations made at three different points in the novel could be placed alongside each other and compared when the novel was finished. Pupils could discuss not just the predictability of events in general, but also when and why their anticipations changed.

The findings

The activity is clearly a matter of personal response and therefore

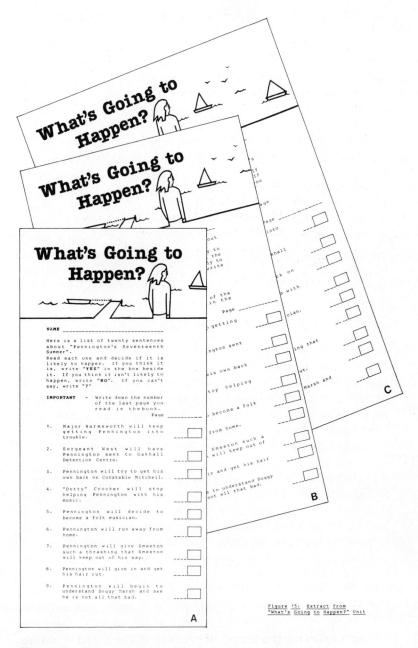

Figure 15: Extract from "What's Going to Happen?" Unit

Figure 15: Extract from 'What's Going to Happen?' Unit

seemed unlikely to be open to any kind of useful quantitative analysis. However, the proportion of 'Can't say' responses proved interesting. We had anticipated that there would be a large number of such responses but we found that pupils were a good deal more confident in their predictions than we expected. In one class of 20 pupils there were only 146 'Can't say' responses out of a possible total of 1200 over three administrations. In another class there were only 137 such responses out of a total of 1140.

More interesting still was the distribution of these 'Can't say' responses across the three administrations. Again we anticipated that as the pupils moved through the novel they would be more able to make firm predictions. They would, after all, have more information to help them. We therefore expected that as they progressed through the novel they would make progressively *fewer* 'Can't say' responses. In one class the figures did show this trend but in the second they did not; in this second class, the number of 'Can't say' responses actually increased as they moved through the novel (9%, 12%, 15%). Notice that these figures are still very low.

We can only speculate as to why some pupils demonstrated increasing uncertainty as they moved through the novel. Most of the pupils could not really explain why they were unsure. Perhaps they became more aware of the complexities of the situation as they read on and realised that the novel was not quite as simple as they at first imagined. Some pupils gave a hint of this in the explanations they offered for their anticipations. For example, in the novel Smeeton and Pennington are enemies and several times Pennington falls victim to his aggression. Item 7 in the 'What's Going to Happen?' unit was as follows:

Pennington will give Smeeton such a thrashing that Smeeton will keep out of his way.'

Since Pennington is described as a powerful youth, he is clearly physically capable of doing this. The majority of pupils seemed to see this as a very likely occurrence. Here is how three pupils justified their answers:

'Yes. Smeeton has been getting at Pennington ever since the story has begun. Pennington, with all his troubles is bound to get fed up of Smeeton. Therefore taking all his troubles and take them out on Smeeton by giving him a thrashing.'

'No. I don't think Pennington will get involved with Smeeton now that he has got a job.'

'I don't know because Pennington is in enough trouble with the police but he still wants to beat him up.'

These pupils are clearly aware of the conflict situation in which Pennington was placed. Their responses are based on knowledge acquired from the novel, combined with more general experience of how people behave in Pennington's circumstances. They imply that Pennington's situation had something of the depth to be found in real-life circumstances. All responses were not of this type – e.g. 'Yes, because he doesn't like him' or 'Yes, because Pennington will want to get his own back' – but they did seem to give something which could be built upon.

Pupils filled in the first anticipation sheet after reading as far as Chapter 3. By the time they had read several more chapters and were filling in the second anticipation sheet, we expected their responses to some items would have changed. Similarly, we expected some changes in responses when filling in the third sheet. (Pupils did not have their previous predictions by them when they filled in a later anticipation sheet.) Since there were 20 items to be attempted 3 times, there were 40 possible changes.

In fact, the number of changes made by individuals ranged from a remarkably low figure of 5 to the highest recorded figure of 23. The tendency to change responses seems to be related to the tendency to use the 'Can't say' response; i.e. pupils who made a lot of changes also responded more often with 'Can't say'. It seems that pupils may differ markedly in the flexibility with which they read a novel. Given that, fairly early on, readers form some sort of opinion about how the story will unfold, some readers appear to be more ready than others to change that opinion as they read further. Possibly those who are less ready to change are the readers who tend to prefer novels with predictable storylines. Although such novels are much criticised, they are read by remarkably large numbers of children and adults.

2.   *Evaluation*

Pupils who read 'The Pit' were asked to complete an 'Evaluation' unit. An extract is reproduced below:

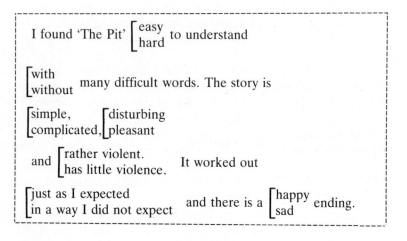

Figure 16:   Extract from 'Evaluation' unit used with 'The Pit'

Teachers reacted in one of two ways to this unit. Approximately half of them regarded it as being fundamentally misguided and unsatisfactory and therefore rejected it. The remainder regarded the 'Evaluation' unit as the least satisfactory of our 'Pit' materials, but welcomed it as a first step towards developing techniques to assess what is acknowledged to be a very difficult area. These teachers reported that some pupils have great difficulty in producing any kind of evaluative statement about what they have read. Such pupils were able to make *some* comment using this evaluation unit.

Our feeling was that the 'Evaluation' unit needed to be tied in more closely with the pupils' understanding and interpretation of the events and characters in the novel. The Personal Response element in novel-reading should not be limited to evaluation activities. We therefore attempted to get pupils to reflect on and make use of responses they had already made to other units. To do this, we introduced 'write-in' sections into the 'Evaluation' unit prepared for 'Pennington'. In these sections, pupils had to support their judgments by citing events and situations from the novel. To do this they could make use of the other assessment units they had already completed.

Here is the section from the 'Pennington Evaluation' unit which corresponds to the extract from the 'Pit' material shown in Figure 16:

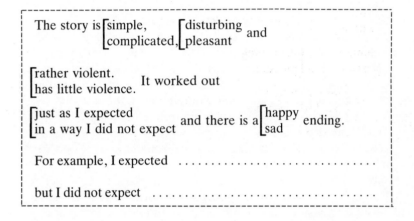

Figure 17: Extract from 'Evaluation' unit used with 'Pennington'

Pupils, then, were asked to give evidence in support of their judgments. As can be seen in Figure 17, they had to state whether the story worked out as they expected. Once they had answered this question, they were asked to elaborate by giving an example of something they expected to happen and then something they did not expect to happen. In the 'What's Going to Happen?' unit pupils had already predicted, at various stages in reading the novel, what they thought was going to happen later. This meant that pupils had something to refer to when answering these evaluative questions. Though only two classes actually used this unit all but three of the thirty-six pupils were able to provide examples. Four responded in very general terms, e.g. they expected the story 'to tell you more about him' or they expected 'something else to happen'. All the others gave specific examples. For example, they expected 'Penn to go to Oakhall' but did not expect 'Penn to go to College'.

Overall, this particular item proved to be unsatisfactory. Nevertheless, it illustrates an important principle in item construction. When constructing sequences of items it is important to consider the consequences that answers given to early items will have for the interpretation of later items. This particular item was reasonably straightforward for pupils who said that the novel had worked out just as they expected. Even then, they had some difficulty in providing a response when asked to nominate an event they did *not* expect. Some of these pupils, quite reasonably, left this part blank. The item was more difficult, however, for those pupils who claimed that the novel did *not* work out as they expected. Many of them failed to recognise the complexities underlying this apparently simple item. We acknowledge that the complexities were unnecessary and they reduced the amount of useful information that could be derived from this section.

Other write-in sections, however, were more satisfactory. The final item in the unit asked pupils whether they thought people could learn a lot or very little about life from the book. (Two thirds of the pupils felt that people could learn a lot about life.) The subsequent write-in section asked for an example of something people might learn. The responses to this section were interesting because they showed different interpretations of what appears to be a simple straightforward question. Some pupils, instead of replying in terms of what might be learned about life, responded in terms of what they learned *about the book*. We did not expect pupils to reply, for example, that 'They would learn it was an interesting story'!

When pupils did answer in terms of what could be learned about life, responses varied from the quite specific to the very general. Answers at the specific level included 'Do not go to school with long hair' or 'You are better to wear your school uniform and your hair neatly cut'. Slightly more general responses were 'To behave themselves' or 'Even if you don't do well in school you could end up with a good trade at the end' or 'They might have to stay on at school if they don't want to.' Several pupils expressed thoughts about life in general rather than about life in school. One pupil felt people could learn 'to keep your wits about you.' Another pupil responded with 'Life is not as easy as some thought' while another said 'Everyone is good at something.'

In this 'Evaluation' unit we asked pupils to justify the

judgements they had made about the novel. In some parts of the unit, we hoped that they would make use of the responses they had made in earlier units. At this point in the project we were not yet aware of the problems that arise in second-level tasks of this nature, i.e. in tasks where pupils are asked to reflect on responses they have already made. These problems were revealed much more clearly when, in a later study, we asked pupils to evaluate a short story. In the meantime, introducing a write-in element into the 'Evaluation' unit was generally agreed to be a step in the right direction.

Conclusions

In attempting to assess pupils' reading of 'Pennington's Seventeenth Summer' we considered it appropriate to apply three techniques devised for use with 'The Pit'. Although minor modifications had to be made, it proved quite feasible to use these techniques to construct assessment units for use with 'Pennington'. In addition a new and more successful form of anticipation exercise was introduced ('What's Going to Happen?' unit) and important changes were made in the 'Evaluation' unit.

'The Pit' differed from 'Pennington's Seventeenth Summer' in several important respects. Some of these seemed to be potential sources of difficulty. New techniques were devised to help teachers to assess the impact on pupils of lengthy descriptive passages and to investigate pupils' appreciation of conflict situations.

Note

Two issues of some importance arose in the course of the novel-reading investigations. The first was that the use of assessment materials should not be seen only as an end-of-novel activity. Most of the assessment materials could be used at different stages during the reading of a novel. Indeed the 'What's Going to Happen?' unit was designed specifically for this purpose.

Secondly, it was clear that 'answers' as such were of relatively little consequence. Pupils' justifications revealed far more about how they were thinking, and were much more relevant to the nature of personal response reading.

By this stage in our work we were becoming very aware that all reading involves making personal responses. It is clear that pupils do not always perceive the task in the way the teacher intends. They respond to a question in terms of their own individual interpretation of it. In formative assessment, therefore, the teacher needs to be sensitive to the way in which the *pupil* interprets a question or understands a task. This mismatch between pupil and teacher in the way they interpret the same question or the same set of instructions is the focus of attention in the next two chapters.

Constructing Formative Assessment Activities for Comprehend-Personal-Response Reading

Here we provide a guide to help teachers construct formative assessment materials for use with Comprehend-Personal Response reading tasks of their own choice.

General Points

In dealing with imaginative literature, there will always be argument over what constitutes an acceptable level of comprehension or what can be regarded as a 'true' reading. The difficulty arises because a reader's understanding of imaginative text is in itself a personal response to that text. Gross misunderstanding is easily recognised, but at other levels what one person sees as a misunderstanding another may accept as an interesting new interpretation. Thus, although it may seem conceptually straightforward to distinguish between Comprehension and Personal Response, in actual practice difficulties will inevitably arise. We would, however, argue that investigation of Personal Response reading should not be confined to assessments which ask for evaluation and appreciation. It is, after all, quite possible for a reader to offer an evaluation or appreciation of a literary text which he or she has misunderstood or only partially comprehended.

Techniques of Item Construction

There are two issues to consider when planning assessment materials for use with a novel. The first is to consider *which aspects of the reading task are to be assessed.* As we have already stated, we have only begun to explore what happens when novels are read. So far we have devised and tried out only a limited range of techniques and have looked at only a handful of the features in novel-reading which may lead pupils into difficulty.

The second issue relates to *when the assessment is to take place.* Formative assessment is an ongoing informal process. Provided the activities are not too intrusive, we believe that some formative assessment procedures should be deployed during the reading of a novel as well as after it has been read. Useful activities may also be introduced *before* the novel is tackled.

The activities we have piloted relate to different aspects of novel-reading. In Diagram 5, we try to show the stages in reading a novel when it may be appropriate to carry out these activities. Several of the units or a sample of items from them can be used either during or after reading the novel. The anticipation unit is essentially a 'during reading' activity though it is profitable for pupils to look back on their decisions after they have completed the novel. In our experience, the conflict resolution activity ('Whose Problem?') is most easily handled after reading the novel. Although the Evaluation Unit can only be carried out after the novel has been read, it is possible to conduct preparatory activities while the novel is being read.

At this stage we do not know enough about what makes an item difficult or easy to be able to offer detailed advice on how to construct actual items. The diagram below may help teachers in thinking about and planning their own formative assessment activities. The range of techniques will, of course, need to be extended to incorporate additional aspects of novel-reading.

Aspect of Novel-Reading	When Assessment Can Be Undertaken	
	While Reading	After Reading
Setting	← 'Pit Country' Unit → ← 'Penn's Patch' Unit →	
Characters	← 'Pit People' Unit → ← 'Pennington People' Unit →	
Plot	← 'Pit Story' Unit → ← 'Pennington Story' Unit →	
Interaction between Plot & Character	'What's Going to Happen?' Unit (Anticipations)	'Whose Problem?' Unit (Conflict)
Overall Evaluation		'Evaluation' Unit

Diagram 5: Matrix showing aspects of novel-reading and stages at which pupils' handling of these aspects can be assessed

CHAPTER 8

Pupils' Perceptions and Teachers' Assumptions:
(1) Reading a Short Story

Introduction

We have remarked several times on the inherent logic of some of the unexpected and, strictly speaking, incorrect answers offered by pupils in response to our reading tasks. Some answers were perfectly sensible in the context of the pupils' perception of the task. Almost invariably, these answers revealed assumptions that we had made about the reading task and about how pupils would tackle it. Teachers will find themselves in a similar position when preparing and using their own materials whether they be for formative or summative assessment. In this chapter and the next we discuss these matters more directly than hitherto. When we embarked on the investigation described in this chapter we were trying to find out about how pupils read short stories. In fact, we learned more about our own assumptions and about pupils' perceptions than we did about the reading of short stories.

Texts Presented in the Context of a Theme

Teachers of English commonly build courses around selected themes. Presenting texts in the context of a theme allows the teacher to encourage two kinds of learning. Firstly, pupils develop knowledge, ideas and personal responses to the constellation of ideas and attitudes which constitute the theme. In other words they can learn *from* the texts. Secondly, working with themes may encourage in pupils an awareness of differences among texts and may help to develop flexible strategies to cope with these. In other words, the pupils learn *about* texts and how to read them. They learn how to read poems, short stories, newspaper articles, novels, song lyrics, advertisements, and so on.

In reading a text there seem to be two phases during which formative assessment procedures might be introduced. We might assess how the pupil reads (the process of reading) or we might assess what he has gained from his reading (the outcome). There are two kinds of reading outcome. One is related to the content of the text (e.g. Has the pupil picked up certain required information from the passage?). The other is related to the kind of writing or text (e.g. Has the pupil learned about the characteristic style or structure of newspaper reports?). Should these outcomes be inadequate or far too laboriously achieved, we would naturally want to look at *how* the pupil tackled the text (the process). Concern about the outcome of pupils' reading leads inevitably to concern about reading processes.

The Short Story Used in the Study

A secondary school gave us the opportunity to put into practice some of the ideas we have just described. Members of the English department were developing a science fiction unit. All the prose texts in the unit of work were imaginative rather than expository and most were complete short stories. We concentrated our efforts on one of the short stories included in the science fiction unit.

The short story we worked with was Arthur Clarke's 'History Lesson'. Although the story had this title in the anthology used by the pupils it is most accessible as 'Expedition to Earth' (Clarke, 1954). A good short story can never be adequately summarised but the attempt which follows may help those who have not read 'History Lesson' to follow the rest of this chapter.

'History Lesson': A Summary

'History Lesson' is based on the idea that the earth's climate is changed so that the polar ice-caps move and expand. The same event which causes the decrease in the earth's temperature increases the temperature on Venus. Over a period of thousands of years, the ice spreads towards the equator, civilisation crumbles and western man reverts to a nomadic existence moving south to escape the ice. Books, pieces of technology, etc. lose their practical significance but are regarded as 'treasures' to be preserved for posterity. Two brief episodes are recounted involving a tribe moving south. The first describes members of the tribe reaching mountains which, they anticipate, will block the southward advance of the ice. On climbing these, they find that the ice has also been moving northwards from the southern pole. In the second episode, members of the succeeding generation are seen burying the 'treasures' on the summit of the mountains in the hope that something will be preserved for posterity. Thousands of years later, Venusians pick up signals from one of the 'treasures', a radio beacon. They land on Earth, find the 'treasures' and return to Venus. In the final episode, leading Venusians are told that while scientists have been able to get nothing from all the other 'treasures', a machine has been constructed (a cine projector) whereby they will at last be able to see from one of the 'treasures' (a reel of film) the creatures who lived on Earth. A Walt Disney cartoon is then shown!

We might look for two kinds of learning as a result of reading this short story. One would be an understanding and appreciation of Clark's ideas and attitudes as embodied in the story. The other would be an increase in pupils' understanding of the nature of short stories and science fiction and in their competence in reading these. We set out to develop formative assessment materials related to both kinds of learning. As always, we tried to devise techniques which could be applied to other similar texts.

Assessment as 'Support'

The 'support' approach to assessment involves investigation of the conditions under which pupils *can* achieve acceptable levels of performance on a task. Knowledge of such conditions gives insight into how development can be encouraged. In our work on form-filling (see Chapter 5) we suggested that useful formative information could be gained by analysing the amount and kind of support pupils needed in order to succeed. We tried to adapt this approach for use with 'History Lesson'.

We felt that support in reading a short story could be offered in several ways and at different points during reading:

(a) Pupils might undertake work before reading the short story to prepare them for the key ideas, or to introduce them to obscure content.

(b) We might help pupils *during* the reading of the story, by using something like the anticipation units described in the last chapter.

(c) We might support them in reflecting on and thinking about the story they have just read.

(d) We might help them to form and present evaluative responses to the story.

In this chapter we concentrate on (c) and (d) above: supporting pupils in studying and reflecting on what they had read and in making evaluative responses to it. This means that we will report only on a selection of the materials we developed, namely Units 2, 3, 4 and 6.

Support in Studying and Reflecting on the Story

In the classes involved in our study, teachers read the story to their pupils who followed it in their own copies. At different points in the story we wanted pupils to anticipate what was going to happen so that they could compare their predictions with what actually happened. Teachers paused at these points and asked pupils to *think about* (not discuss) what might happen next. This, of course, offered direction *while* reading the story as suggested in (b) above.

We wanted pupils, while reflecting on the story, to think about what Beck et al. (1979) call the story plan, i.e. the key elements in the story. This may not be particularly important as an end in itself but it is usually a necessary preliminary to understanding the content and ideas. We felt that, in 'History Lesson', it might be more difficult than usual to pick up the conventional story structure, since in this story none of the characters present in earlier episodes is also present in the later episodes. This means that there is no unifying character or characters who respond to or control events throughout the story. It seemed appropriate, therefore, to introduce a task which asked pupils to identify the four episodes in the story and to think about the connections between them.

The Materials

'History Lesson' is divided into four episodes, which are separated by unusually long periods of time (a generation or even thousands of years). We felt that pupils might need support in recognising the presence and extent of these episodes and in retaining the sequence. We therefore devised the task reproduced in Figures 18 and 19.

In most stories things happen in a short time: a day, a week, a year or a few years. The story in 'History Lesson' takes *thousands of years*. The chart on the next page tries to show this.

Four points on the chart are marked with circles. These stand for the episodes in the story when we are told exactly what people are doing. What happened during these episodes? The first one is done for you.

(A)   Shann and his two sons climb the mountain.

(B)

(C)

(D)

Figure 18:   Unit 2: Identifying and Sequencing Episodes

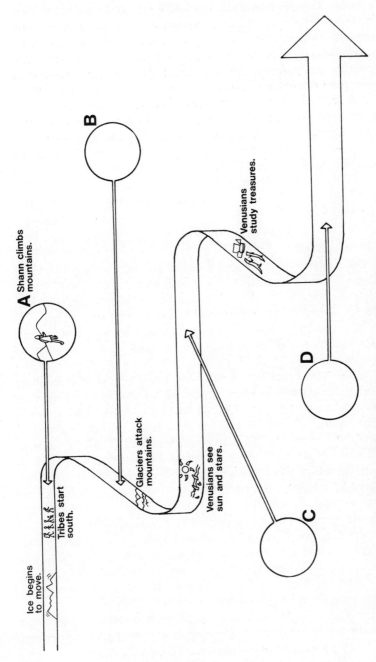

A Shann climbs mountains.

B

Ice begins to move.

Tribes start south.

Glaciers attack mountains.

Venusians see sun and stars.

C

Venusians study treasures.

D

Figure 19: Unit 2: Diagram used to Identify Episodes in 'History Lesson'

In this task the pupils had to consider the structure of the story in terms of its four basic episodes. We then had to devise possible ways of supporting the pupils' comprehension of what happens *within* each episode.

Singer & Donlan (1982) have produced an interesting study of how pupils might be instructed in the 'active comprehension' of short stories. They argue that, because short stories have certain features in common, there is a set of key, generic questions which can be pertinently asked of all short stories. These include:

Who is the leading character?
What is the leading character trying to accomplish?
What obstacles does the character encounter en route to a goal?
Does the character reach the goal?

These questions relate to key elements found in almost all short stories, namely character, goal, obstacle and outcome. These generic questions would, of course, have to be translated into specific terms for each individual story. In their study, Singer & Donlan produce evidence to suggest that training pupils to ask such questions of themselves while reading is beneficial to comprehension.

We do not know how valid is their description of how short stories are comprehended. Indeed, as presented by Singer & Donlan, the pattern seems rather too conventional. On the other hand, appreciation of the unusual in literature may depend on our awareness of how it differs from the standard. These authors do offer one of the few theoretically based and systematic guides to question-setting *which takes account of the nature of the text*. Many taxonomies have been prepared to help teachers set questions on passages (e.g. Barrett, 1968; Guszak, 1972) but they tend to ignore kind of text as a factor in questioning. For example, teachers may feel that a 'good' set of questions should include some which demand inferences, regardless of whether such questions are important for understanding the particular text to be read. Note also that the Singer & Donlan approach is designed to produce questions which help the pupil to understand the text.

It seemed worthwhile, therefore, to base a study task on these questions if, in fact, they were relevant to the story we were using.

We did feel that the questions had relevance for 'History Lesson', but at the level of episode rather than at the level of the complete story. In Unit 3, shown in Figure 20, the questions set on each episode were based on this approach. (The unit heading and the spaces for answers have been removed to allow all the questions to be reproduced on a single page.) Note that the wording of the unit assumes that pupils will use it just after completing Unit 2.

The questions set for each episode follow a standard pattern. The first question asks the reader to recall (or identify) the principal characters, the second asks the reader to consider the aims or goals of these characters and the third relates to the obstacles which prevent the goals being attained. The fourth question asks the reader to reflect on what he anticipated the outcome would be and thus leads into the next episode. Although our questions do in some cases contain direct references to the story 'History Lesson', we aimed to formulate questions in fairly general terms so that with little modification, they could be applied (by teacher and reader) to other short stories.

The questions we set were not intended to be in any way searching. Their function was to help readers 'review' what they had read before moving on to evaluation and appreciation. If readers are asked the same basic question on a series of stories or on the episodes within a story, they may develop a general strategy which can be useful when reading other similar texts. In due course they may come to apply the strategy without support. It was hoped that the questions would provoke the pupils into the kind of text processing which an active reader would engage in while reading the story. Of course, a fluent reader would be unlikely to formulate the questions consciously.

Our materials, then, included two units which were intended to prompt pupils to use particular strategies when reflecting on or reviewing the text. Unit 2 attempted to induce readers to perceive and use the episodic structure of the overall story. In Unit 3 we tried to direct readers' attention to the common structure of the episodes by introducing a standard pattern of questions for each one. Naturally, we did not expect pupils to adopt this strategy for themselves as the result of reading only one short story. We have no means of knowing how many stories would have to be read to produce any such effect. Some of our findings may, however, be useful.

We thought that these were the four episodes in 'History Lesson' when we are told what people were doing:
  (A)   At the Mountain Pass
  (B)   At the Cairn
  (C)   Circling Earth
  (D)   At the Meeting
Now try to remember each of these episodes and answer these questions.

(A) **At the Mountain Pass**
  1.   Who are the main characters in this episode?
  2.   Why are they wanting to reach the mountains?
  3.   What upset their hopes?
  4.   Try to remember what you were thinking when you read this episode for the first time. What did you think was going to happen when they set off to climb the mountain?

(B) **At the Cairn**
  1.   Who are the main characters in this episode?
  2.   Why are they burying their 'treasures'?
  3.   What did they fear would upset their plan?
  4.   When you were reading this episode for the first time, what did you think would happen next? Did you expect Venusians to appear?

(C) **Circling the Earth**
  1.   Who are the main characters in this episode?
  2.   Why were they circling the Earth?
  3.   What changed their plan?
  4.   What did you think might happen next?

(D) **At the Meeting**
  1.   Who is the main character in this episode?
  2.   What have the Venusians been trying to do since the Earth landing?
  3.   What upset their plan?
  4.   What have they done to overcome their problems?
  5.   What do they plan to do in the years to come?
  6.   What do you know will upset their plans?
  7.   What did you expect to happen at the end of the meeting?

Figure 20:   Unit 3: Review questions for episodes in 'History Lesson'

The findings

1. STRATEGY PROMPTING

In Units 2 and 3 we tried to prompt pupils to use particular reading strategies which seemed appropriate for reading short stories. In early pilot trials, both of these units proved to be difficult and so they were subsequently modified. As a result of these modifications there was a substantial improvement in pupils' performance. Unfortunately, this improvement did not seem to be the result of a change in the way pupils read the short story.

In the original version of Unit 2 pupils had to identify the four episodes in the story and plot them on a time chart. In the modified version episodes were identified for pupils and presented in random order. Pupils were again asked to plot them on the time chart. Those who tackled the unit in its revised form were more successful than those who used the original version. Thus by modifying the unit we were able to increase the success rate – but in so doing we changed the nature of the task itself. We were not aware of this, however, when we introduced the modification.

In Unit 3 we were also able to raise the proportion of 'correct' answers by 'improving' the questions. Our modifications involved signalling more clearly how and where the questions related to the text. For example, changing one question from 'What changed their plan?' to 'Why did they change their plan and land?' almost doubled the proportion of correct answers given. However, what we did not realise was that, as with Unit 2, we had changed the nature of the assessment task. Questions had not simply been made clearer; they now indicated the parts of the text in which the answers could be found.

This had an important effect on how pupils answered questions. Whether giving right or wrong answers, pupils now showed an increased tendency to answer by giving direct quotation or a simple paraphrase. Compared with pupils who tackled the unit in its original form, a smaller proportion now answered in their own words. Answers in the form of quotations or paraphrases are arrived at by searching the text rather than by recalling the story.

We think that answering the 'improved' questions involved different kinds of processes from those needed to answer the questions when they were phrased in a more general form, less closely tied to the text. The increased success with the modified questions seems to have been achieved by prompting pupils to make use of question-answering strategies rather than story-reading strategies. We would therefore argue that, in formative assessment, the teacher must be aware that a question-answering strategy rather than a reading strategy may be operating. When the reader does not fully understand the story or the question, he or she may set out to find and then quote or paraphrase parts of the text which appear in some way to be connected with the question. Indeed, it is sometimes possible to detect the point when a pupil switches from a reading strategy to a question-answering strategy.

2.   RETROSPECTIVE QUESTIONING

Unit 3 consisted of 'review' material designed to help pupils reflect on what they had just read. The material (reproduced in Figure 20) consisted of a series of questions to be answered retrospectively, after the *complete* story had been read. Our findings suggest that this kind of retrospective questioning is more demanding than is often acknowledged and is particularly demanding when pupils find a story difficult. We further hypothesise that in these circumstances retrospective questioning produces its own kinds of error and, more specifically, may have the following two effects:

(a) Pupils often answer early questions with information which would provide the appropriate answers to later questions. Having once used an answer, pupils are reluctant to use it again.

(b) Having read the story, pupils find it difficult to distinguish between what characters *intended* to do and what, in the long run, they actually *did* do.

Neither of these problems would arise if questions were presented and answered at appropriate intervals while reading the story. The first of these effects will be familiar to most teachers. The second is less frequently commented on and perhaps less easily identified but an example should make clear what we mean.

In answering the questions on the first episode of 'History

Lesson' (Questions A, 1–4 in Figure 20) pupils often suggested that the members of the tribe were trying to reach the mountains to bury their treasures (what actually happened) rather than to escape from the ice (their intention). Similarly, in answering the questions on the third episode, some pupils said the Venusians were landing to find the treasures (what actually happened) rather than to identify the source of a radio signal (their intention). These types of error may be an artefact of retrospective questioning. In such questioning the convention is to set questions in a sequence that will take readers back to the beginning and lead them through the story or passage again. When answering questions early in the sequence, therefore, the reader must temporarily *hold in abeyance* some of the information which was acquired from the later parts of the story. This is a feat we take for granted and one which may not be a necessary accompaniment to comprehension as such. Failure to give satisfactory answers to retrospective questions does not necessarily mean that there has been a failure of ongoing comprehension during the reading of the story.

These comments should not be read as an attack on retrospective questioning. Rather, they argue for recognition of the demands this technique makes on a pupil's awareness of and control over his own thinking processes. Effective formative assessment will recognise that pupils have to observe rather peculiar conventions when answering questions set in this way. Reading a lengthy piece of text is a cumulative process by which the reader builds up a representation of what is contained in the text. It is a major assumption that readers who have successfully comprehended the text will also be able to unravel their representation in such a way that they can isolate key elements and review them in sequence to provide answers to retrospective questions.

Support in Evaluating the Story

Evaluating a text is generally acknowledged to be a high level activity. There are at least two reasons why pupils find it difficult to produce evaluations of texts they have read. Firstly, they may not know what kinds of things they should attend to and comment on. Secondly, they may find it difficult to put their thoughts and feelings into words.

The materials

Two units (Units 4 and 6) aimed to produce evaluative thinking about 'History Lesson'. In both of these units we tried to confront pupils with some of the issues in this particular story which we thought were worthy of comment. At the same time we wanted to reduce the burden involved in formulating a response. To do this we offered pupils questions or statements to which they were asked to give YES/NO or AGREE/DISAGREE responses. We used these binary-choice formats because pupils would find it easy to offer a response. The weaknesses of binary-choice items are well known (Popham, 1981). Among the most important of these is that the same answer can be given for quite different reasons. Nevertheless, analysis of the justifications pupils give for their responses yields useful formative information. We were interested, therefore, not so much in the answers themselves as in the explanations pupils subsequently offered for these answers.

The materials we prepared to encourage evaluative thinking about the story asked for responses to two different kinds of statements. In Unit 4 pupils had to consider statements they themselves had produced. The unit consisted of three sections which were designed to draw attention respectively to the insignificance of the characters in the story, to the overall air of pessimism throughout and to the futility of the actions described. We hoped that these would lead pupils to start to build an evaluation of the story. Instead of asking pupils to generate comments on these matters, we asked them to refer back to and reflect on the answers they had already given to the questions in Unit 3. They had to take a decision about these responses and respond in YES/NO terms. An extract from this unit is reproduced as Figure 21 on page 136.

In Unit 6 we tried to lead pupils to consider more of the issues relevant to an evaluation of 'History Lesson'. Whereas in Unit 4 pupils were reflecting on statements *they themselves had produced* as answers, this time *we provided* a series of statements about the story and asked pupils to indicate whether they agreed or disagreed with them. The statements were presented in groups, each group focusing on a different issue. It was hoped that, by using more than one item related to each issue, consistent patterns of responding could be detected. The examples we use to illustrate our findings relate to two of these issues.

(a) Did pupils appreciate why the author selected these particular 'treasures'?

(b) In this story did pupils appreciate the ironic commentary on the way inferences are made on the basis of limited evidence?

The findings

As might be expected, pupils who offered the same answer to a given item did so for quite different reasons. We do not propose to elaborate further on this finding as it is well documented in the literature on binary-choice items. Much more relevant to formative assessment is a consideration of why these differences arose. Our contention is that the most significant source of differences was the level at which the pupils interpreted the item or the story. We now try to illustrate what we mean by differences in level of interpretation.

1. RESPONDING TO ACTUAL WORDS RATHER THAN MEANING
The first part of Unit 4 is reproduced in Figure 21. Each episode in the story introduces a change in the principal character or agent and we had identified this as a possible source of difficulty. Shann (and his sons) are the main characters in the first episode, Shann's sons in the second, the Venusian space-ship crew in the third and the Venusian Historian in the final episode. Question 1 in each section of Unit 3 – 'Who is/are the main character(s) in this episode?' – had been intended to draw attention to these changes. The first question in Unit 4 (see Figure 21) required pupils to look back at their answers and note that the main characters change in each episode.

When using Unit 3, a pupil gave the following answer to the first question on Episode 1:

'Shann and his tribe people'

To the first question on Episode 2 he gave the answer:

'Shann and his tribe folk'

You will need to use your answers to Sheet 3 to help you do this one (see Figure 20).

Maybe you thought that 'History Lesson' seemed different from other short stories you have read in school.

On Sheet 3, look at your *answers* to the *first question* in each of sections A, B, C and D. These questions were about the characters.

Did you give a different answer to each of these first questions? Write YES or NO. . . . .

Do you feel you know much about the characters in 'History Lesson'? Write YES or NO. . . . .

Figure 21:   Unit 4: 'History Lesson' materials

When working on Unit 4 (Figure 21), the pupil asserted that these answers were different. Our question had been intended to probe at the level of meaning but this pupil, like many others, based his decision on the actual words used in the answers rather than on the content referred to in those answers. Although the pupil maintained that these answers were different, mature readers would see them as being the same.

Let us consider another example. In Unit 3 many pupils identified 'Shann and his sons' as the main characters in Episode 1 and 'Shann's sons' as the equivalent in Episode 2. These answers were correct. Shann had died and a generation had passed between the two episodes. Some pupils, however, adopted a very literal interpretation of the question and held that these answers were the same. In fact they are quite different despite the fact that two out of the three characters appear in both answers. Once again, pupils appear to be operating at the level of actual words used rather than at the level of meaning.

2.   DIFFERENT LEVELS OF INTERPRETATION: THE STORY

In the story the members of the tribe bury their 'treasures' in the hope that something will be preserved for posterity. On the face of it, there is something ludicrous in describing a collection of broken odds and ends as 'treasures'. The force of the label 'treasures' is only appreciated when the ironic quality of the story is grasped.

In Unit 6 pupils were invited to agree or disagree with statements about the author's choice of 'treasures'.

Item 7:   The author was silly to say that things like a broken lens or a cutter from an electric razor could be 'treasures'.

Item 8:   For this story, the author chose the right kinds of things for 'treasures'.

Item 9:   The author should have made the 'treasures' things that were sure to give the correct ideas about human beings.

We expected pupils who had understood the story to disagree with Item 7, agree with Item 8 and disagree with Item 9. Pupils' responses to these items show different levels of understanding of the story. A number of pupils agreed with Item 7, suggesting that they had misunderstood the story. They felt that the author had been unfortunate in his choice of 'treasures'. Here is one pupil's explanation of why he agreed that the author's choice of treasures was 'silly'.

> 'I didn't see what use they would have for a broken lens. They might not know if it's supposed to be broken or not.'

This pupil's immediate response to the item suggested that he had not fully understood the story, and the explanation he subsequently gave for his response confirmed this. He appears to be thinking at a level below that at which the item was directed. In his response he shows no consideration of the function of the 'treasures' in the story. Note, however, that his explanation is quite consistent with his initial agreement that 'the author was silly to say things like a broken lens or a cutter from an electric razor could be "treasures".'

In contrast, there were pupils who recognised, first, that the 'treasures' had a vital function in the story and, second, that this function would not have been served if the treasures had been a more 'conventional' selection. Here are some comments produced by these pupils:

'It wouldn't be much of a good story then',

'The story wouldn't make sense if the treasures gave the right idea about humans. I think the point of the story was to tell you that things could happen like that.'

'There wid be nae pint in't'

Pupils who made this kind of response had to consider and integrate several complex ideas. These pupils were clearly working at a higher level than the pupil whose response was described in the previous paragraph.

We have used these examples to illustrate extreme positions. Our final example is a comment which shows some consideration of the story but falls short of an appreciation of the function of the 'treasures'. The pupil was explaining her response to Item 8: 'For this story, the author chose the right kinds of things for "treasures" '.

She agreed with the statement and explained:

'Well, that's the kind of things they might take for treasures, and they are light things to carry because they had to walk quite far.'

She has appreciated that in the prevailing circumstances 'treasures' would have to be portable. This explanation fits the context of the story though not the author's purpose in writing it.

3. DIFFERENT LEVELS OF INTERPRETATION: THE ITEMS

One group of items in Unit 6 dealt with a central theme in the story, namely that great care must be taken in interpreting evidence. (The Venusians were about to construct an impression of life on Earth by studying a Walt Disney cartoon.) We provided a group of statements featuring people whose daily occupation requires them to handle evidence. Pupils had to indicate if such individuals would benefit from reading the story. For example, in one item pupils had to consider whether 'People who dig up and study things like old bones, coins and pots should learn a special lesson from this story.'

This group of items was very demanding because it required pupils to operate at a high conceptual level. Here are some of the comments offered by pupils who disagreed with the statement:

> 'It's nothing really to do with people who dig up old coins and things in the story.'

> 'If they dig up coins and everything, how are they going to learn from the story? The story doesn't tell you about coins and everything – just things for folk to find when they come to the planet.'

> 'It was all modern things they left behind.'

Notice how, in the last response, the fact that modern things were used as 'treasures' means that the story can have no relevance for people who study 'old' things. In their thinking, these pupils have not moved beyond the specifics in the item.

As a result of the same kind of thinking, several pupils disagreed with the following statement: 'People who study history should learn a special lesson from this story.'

Typical comments included:

> 'How can you learn about history from something about the future? It's an impossibility. It can't be done.'

> 'It's not a true story. History is meant to be truthful. They wouldn't really learn 'cause it hasn't happened.'

The pupils' logic is impeccable but their concept of history is inadequate for this particular task.

The explanations pupils gave for their responses to the items in these two units produced useful information. YES/NO or AGREE/DISAGREE items have the advantage of quickly eliciting a response to be justified. The answers themselves, however, can be extremely misleading. This is because too often pupils are *not* answering the question the assessor intended to ask but another interpretation of it. Both when reflecting on statements they themselves had made and when reflecting on statements provided by others, many pupils responded at the level of specifics and not at the higher level of generality necessary for understanding the items or the story. Evaluation of any text requires a level of thinking that goes beyond a consideration of specific features.

Conclusions

The work reported in this chapter forced us to recognise three problems which beset both summative and formative assessment. The first is the problem of recognising difficulties inherent in the assessment techniques used. We assumed that retrospective questioning would lead pupils to a deeper understanding of a story they had just read and would place them in a better position to evaluate it. However, we did not recognise the quite severe demands which the retrospective element in this technique seems to place on pupils who have found a story difficult. An assessment technique may present few problems when used with a text which is well within a pupil's competence to comprehend. The difficulties inherent in the nature of the technique may only become apparent when the technique is used in relation to a text which is outwith or at the extreme limit of that pupil's comprehension. We know very little about the relative difficulty of the different techniques used in the assessment of reading. Indeed, it may not be possible to talk about the difficulty of a particular reading assessment technique without taking into account the degree of correspondence that exists between the text and the reader's competence to comprehend it. For example, the common assertion that cloze procedure can be difficult may be a reflection of a mismatch between text difficulty and reader competence. Cloze procedure, as an assessment technique, may be unsuitable for use when a pupil is pushed to the limit of his reading capacity.

This investigation highlighted a second problem for teachers conducting formative assessment. The fact that pupils have given correct answers to a series of questions does not necessarily demonstrate that they have understood the text. It may be that the assessment items are such that it is possible for a pupil to arrive at the right answers without understanding the text. In Unit 3 we tried to provide a series of very general questions which we hoped would help pupils to *reflect* not only on 'History Lesson' but also on other similar short stories. We very soon recognised that pupils were having difficulty in understanding questions phrased in such general terms. We therefore made the questions more specific while still intending to help pupils to reflect on what they had read. In doing this, however, we produced questions which could now be answered without understanding and reviewing the story. Our modifications made it possible for pupils to treat the task as a series of discrete questions to be answered by focusing on particular sentences or phrases in the text. Pupils who might have found it difficult to relate the general questions to the story were now able to deploy well-practised, question-answering strategies which can produce right answers without a full understanding of the text as a whole.

The third problem concerns the level at which the reader chooses to interpret the text or the assessment item. We have given several examples of how pupils interpreted the story and the items at a level lower than or different from that which we intended. In the next chapter, we try to take this matter further. What do pupils spontaneously attend to in a text? How might teachers lead them to attend to particular higher level features and themes?

CHAPTER 9

Pupils' Perceptions and Teachers' Assumptions:
(2) Recognising 'Kinds' of Text

Introduction

In Chapter 8 we argued that by presenting texts in the context of a theme or topic teachers can hope to encourage two developments: development in the understanding of the ideas and attitudes connected with the theme and development in the competence with which the different kinds of text are handled. Encouraging these developments will involve fostering in pupils an awareness of the different types of writing represented in a particular collection of texts as well as helping them to recognise the common thread of idea and argument running through that collection.

Developing pupils' ability to recognise and respond to similarities and differences among texts seems to be implicit in a thematic approach to teaching English. Clearly the 'themes' themselves cannot be of central importance. If they were, English teachers would not have such freedom in selecting themes and in choosing texts. Rather, it is the experience of reflecting on and responding to a collection of texts, tapes, etc. and developing a competence in doing this which seems to be vital. In terms of reading, progressive sophistication in perceiving similarities and differences among different pieces of writing does seem to be an important, if sometimes unconscious, aim in English teaching. These similarities and differences may be at the level of content, of presentation or of purpose.

The need for pupils to be aware of similarities and differences among texts was implicit also in the organisation of more traditional English teaching. An older generation of English teachers used genre as the shared characteristic and timetabled classes for poetry, for work on the novel and for drama. Under the old regime pupils met texts from the same genre and discovered differences in topic or theme: under the new regime they meet texts related to the same topic or theme and discover differences in genre.

Categorising Texts

In the course of this research project we have distinguished among different kinds of reading tasks. We have described Search-Do reading tasks (using telephone directories and dictionaries), Comprehend-Do reading tasks (understanding sets of directions and filling in forms) and Comprehend-Personal-Response reading (reading novels and short stories). In studying these kinds of reading tasks, we had no difficulty in deciding which kind of text to use. For example, when we had to consider pupils' ability to read and make a personal response to texts, we turned to novels and short stories. We might also have used poems or plays. Similarly, in studying Search-Do reading we turned to telephone directories and dictionaries since they are typical of a whole range of texts which are basically lists. Thus, in developing a framework for categorising reading tasks, we inadvertently produced a way of categorising texts. In our case, categorisation was in terms of suitability for assessing performance on different kinds of reading tasks. Without denying that there are important differences, we stress the similarities between consulting telephone directories and looking up dictionaries, between following directions on medicine labels and completing travel booking forms, and between reading a novel like 'The Pit' and a more sophisticated one such as 'Pennington's Seventeenth Summer'. Our questioning strategy on 'History Lesson' is based on the idea that similarities exist among short stories. It is these similarities which, in some respects, permit a common approach.

There are other important and more familiar ways in which adults distinguish between different kinds of writing. Thinking in terms of categories seems to be a feature of mature reading at a quite general level. For example, adults make a fundamental distinction between fact and fiction. Factual reports and fictitious accounts offer different kinds of insight and satisfaction. At a more specialist level these categories can be further subdivided. Factual texts can be grouped into reference books and expository texts; fiction breaks down into science fiction, thrillers, romances and so on.

Different professions make distinctions among texts to serve their own particular purposes. For example, historians differentiate between primary and secondary written sources; scientists distinguish between theoretical and experimental papers. Students of literature make distinctions of increasing refinement; narrative and lyrical poetry, epic and romance, Petrarchan and Elizabethan sonnets. The list of categories is almost endless.

The existence of such categories reflects the fact that authors differ in their intentions, that readers must respond differently to different kinds of text, and that different criteria are required in evaluating different kinds of writing. For example, we expect newspaper reports or textbooks to contain only accurate information. Inaccuracies are unequivocally a major flaw. On the other hand, we do not condemn a novel or a poem because it incorporates errors of, say, historical or scientific fact. Even among novels, however, tolerance for inaccuracies is much less in historical and modern 'documentary' fiction than it is in, say, fantasy or romance. The authors' intentions are different, the readers' responses must be different and different kinds of novels must be judged on different criteria.

Themes and Categories in Teaching English

Since categorising texts is found in so many disciplines, we hypothesised that the ability to recognise similarities and differences among texts might be quite fundamental to mature, reflective reading. How, after all, do teachers and students of English arrive at their responses to poems, novels etc. which they have not read before? Arguably, it is because they 'know' what kinds of things to look for. They 'know' how to read a poem.

We do not really know what this knowledge consists of or how it is acquired. It may be, however, that 'experts' proceed by making a series of unconscious comparisons with other poems and novels with which they are already familiar. To the extent that a poem is typical of its genre, they know what aspects to attend to; to the extent that it is unique within their experience of the genre, they know what special features are worth commenting on. But it is not only genre against which a text can be viewed. It can be considered in relation to other works by the same author or against the background of the period in which the author wrote. Reading a poem within a variety of frameworks generates a richer, fuller response. For example, Chaucer's 'Troilus' can be seen as part of the classical tradition in English literature, in the context of Chaucer's own literary development, as a medieval poem, as the first English novel or as an exploration of courtly love themes. The development of mature and reflective reading may result from learning to view a text within a variety of changing contexts. We do not know how pupils learn to do this, yet a great deal of the teaching that takes place in English classes presupposes an ability to do so.

Pupils with little experience of a particular reading task will need support if they are going to work out for themselves the major points on which they must focus. Their failure to produce an 'adequate' response may be due basically to an ignorance of the rules by which the particular reading 'game' is played. If we are to encourage the development of the ability to identify relevant features in a text then we need some means of discovering those features in texts to which pupils spontaneously attend.

Suppose a class is working on a unit of work on 'Crime and Punishment'. If left to their own devices, will all pupils in fact notice that each passage included in the unit relates to this theme? More important, will the pupils go beyond this? Will they see, for example, that although two passages are concerned with the same topic or theme, the authors are saying different, and perhaps even contradictory, things about it? We suspect that when pupils meet texts in the context of a theme, special demands are made on the ability to see similarities and differences among texts. Evidence from more general psychological studies of how children learn to categorise suggests that competence in categorising texts may, in fact, be quite difficult to attain.

Is an awareness of some of the more elementary categories of text useful, or even necessary, if a reader is to make an appropriate response to a piece of writing? We felt that the whole area was worth studying. In this chapter we report on two exploratory investigations. In the first, which we now describe, we looked for the features on which pupils spontaneously focused when looking at texts. In this investigation we used a 'sorting' task.

'Sorting' as an Assessment Technique

Sorting tasks are quite familiar to school pupils. Infants make considerable use of sorting trays. 'Sets' are introduced in the mid-primary years and are taught as the formal foundations for mathematics in early secondary. Yet, sorting (or grouping or categorising) has not featured very frequently in the teaching of reading or in the teaching of English. (See, however, Gerhard, 1975 and Henry, 1974.) Sulzby (1981), in a study of spelling, asked children to sort words in different ways and, from their performance, deduced how they saw differences and similarities among words. We tried to use Sulzby's 'sorting' technique as a means of investigating how pupils arrive at categories of text.

Sulzby distinguished between 'open' sorts and 'closed' sorts. In an open sort the pupils were allowed to sort the words in any way they liked. The sort was spontaneous. The results of the sort were recorded in the child's notebook and then the child was asked to try to sort them in another way. Writing down the pupil's response stresses that the child's idea is important. In a closed sort, the teacher told the pupil how to make the sort (e.g. 'Find all the words that begin with . . . ') or supported him in some other way. We used both open and closed sorts in our work.

The Passage Sorting Investigation

The object of the exercise was to gain some insight into the kind of categories pupils would naturally use in sorting written passages. Although we did not expect that pupils would use the same categories as a mature reader might, we tried to ensure that a number of these categories were represented in the collection of passages. We used sixteen passages in all, each one printed on a separate card. We thought that subject matter might be a fairly obvious and easy basis on which to begin sorting and so ten passages were about dogs, five were about cats and one was about an otter. We included factual and fictitious passages, poems, an extract from a 'glossary of "canine terms" ', the blurb on the back of a paperback novel, and so on. Two of the 'dog' passages seemed clearly mythological. In another passage, a dog describes how it should be looked after. This was included to provoke discussion about whether the passage belonged to the fiction or non-fiction category.

To familiarise them with the content of the cards pupils undertook a preliminary matching task. The passages from ten of the cards were 'split' in half, and the two parts printed on separate cards. The pupils were presented with the first part of each passage and asked to find the concluding part. This exercise in itself produced interesting information.

In the full sorting task, we expected that pupils might well begin by separating the passages about dogs from the passages about cats. These two groupings seemed fairly obvious. The passages had been so selected that from this simple beginning a more mature categorisation could still result. If pupils separated the 'dog' passages from the others, we planned to ask them to carry out a further sort of the 'dog' passages only. A possible progression through several sorts is outlined in Figure 22 on page 148.

This, then, is a possible categorisation scheme. As will be seen later, spontaneous sorting produced rather different sets of categories. At this stage we simply make the point that various groupings of these passages were possible and that groupings could be made in a hierarchical fashion with superordinate and subordinate categories.

The study was undertaken with a class of primary school pupils aged ten to twelve years. This gave us the opportunity to spend a considerable length of time with each pupil as necessary. Tighter timetabling makes it difficult to undertake this kind of exploratory work in secondary schools.

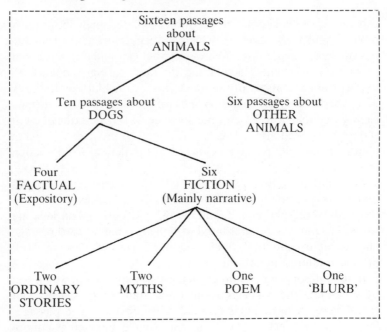

Figure 22:   A Possible Categorisation of Texts

The findings

Pupils tended to produce four or five groups of passages with a small number of passages in each group. Indeed more than half the groupings consisted of only two passages. This evidence raises a question about secondary pupils. To what extent will they, when studying a theme, be able to attend to features which run across a large collection of texts.

The ways in which the primary pupils justified their groupings were as follows:

(a) They referred to specific details or words which appeared in the passages. For example:

'No. 5 says something about kings. No. 7 says something about kings. I just got a quick glance and they say something about kings.'

(b) They retold or summarised the passages. For example:

'No. 3 is that a dog pays no attention to a hen and goes off and does other things instead of watching the hen. No. 11 is that puppies are supposed to be out to play with their mum and they just lie down and are lazy and ignore their mother.'

Sometimes pupils had, in fact, perceived a common feature but did not make this clear in their retelling. In this particular case the pupil was prompted with 'So the thing that links these two is?' He replied 'That they're paying no attention.' In other instances, however, pupils were not able to go beyond a simple retelling.

(c) They referred to shared characteristics of the texts rather than to common content:

'Stories about animals – they're not fiction. They're not stories – they're telling you about subjects.'

'They are poems and an index. They are not stories.'

'I think these are all make up stories – stories about fiction.'

(d) They identified common topics or ideas:

'In both paragraphs someone was needing something. In the first one it was a dog – it needed a dog's basket. In the second one the boy wants the dog.'

Conclusions

We drew three conclusions from the evidence provided by the sorting tasks.

1. Pupils paid attention to several kinds of features. Included among these were ideas *in* the text and ideas *about* the kind of text.

2. In about 90% of groups, the passages were grouped by ideas. Yet both teachers and specialists in reading have long puzzled over the problem of how pupils can be led to perceive and

work on the ideas and in particular the *main* ideas in a passage. The evidence here suggests that pupils who are given a global task like this do tend to respond at the level of ideas. However, the common ideas on which pupils focus are often not what the mature reader would regard as significant.

3.   Teachers cannot assume that a particular textual feature, however salient to them, will appear significant to their pupils. Pupils have to learn what to look for in texts. Many of the tasks set in everyday classwork *assume* that this learning has already taken place.

A Less Time-Consuming Technique

The passage sorting technique proved a useful way of gaining insight into how pupils perceived similarities and differences between passages. It allowed us to identify some unexamined assumptions which we had made, and which teachers may also be in danger of making. The technique, however, was too time-consuming to be used regularly, especially within a normal secondary school timetable. For classroom purposes we required a modified technique which would be practicable in terms of pupil and teacher time, which teachers could apply to texts of their own choosing and which they could use to direct pupils' attention to significant features in a text. We tried to modify the technique to meet these requirements.

The grouping process is essential to the technique. By comparing and contrasting passages, pupils reveal the dimensions on which they are operating. It was obvious, however, that the number of passages used had to be reduced: but how far could we go in this direction? We think that the process can be investigated using only *three* passages. An example will help to make the point. Figure 23 shows a triplet devised to be used with very young children. (Notice that one of the more appealing aspects of this 'triplet' technique is that it can be adapted for pupils at almost any level of development in reading, and with regard to almost any aspect of reading.)

A.   'One day Dick went to the shop with his Mum. He saw a red car in the window. He stopped to look at it. When he turned round his Mum had gone.'

B.   'Dick went to the seaside. The sea was very cold but the sun was warm. He made a big sand castle. The sea came in and washed it away.'

C.   'Jane and Peter were playing hide and seek. Jane ran into the woods to hide. She ran and ran. She waited for someone to find her. No one came. It was getting dark.'

Figure 23:   Three Passages for Use in a 'Triplet'

How might this triplet be used? There are two important dimensions to consider. The first is the *content*. In Passages A and B the same characters appear in different situations. The second dimension is the matter of *theme*. Passages A and C are both about children getting lost, but the characters are different and the setting is different. We suggest that it would be possible to provide pupils with several triplets constructed along these two dimensions. Their groupings might reveal a consistent pattern of responding.

When pupils have made and explained a first grouping using a given triplet, it would be useful to ask them to look again at the same three passages to see if they can find another way in which two of the passages would 'go together'. Doing this has two advantages. Firstly, those pupils who had considered but then rejected one grouping in favour of another would get the opportunity to demonstrate that they had seen an alternative way of grouping the passages. Secondly, it demands a degree of flexibility in the way that pupils respond to texts.

It seemed to us that in English classes, pupils were being asked to look at passages in different ways according to the purpose a teacher had in mind. This was clear from the fact that teachers sometimes used the same passage in different units of work. This is as it should be; there is no one way to 'see' a passage. We doubt, however, if teachers have yet solved the problem of how to develop this flexibility in their pupils. The triplet technique might help to assess it and, as we hope with all our materials, might form the basis of an approach to teaching.

Using the Triplet Technique

We undertook four exploratory studies using the triplet technique. Each study investigated whether pupils could be helped to look at complete texts and to perceive higher order relationships between them. In the first study we investigated whether the technique could be used to help pupils to recognise a common theme. In the second we investigated how the technique might be used to highlight a common style of presentation. The third and fourth studies were concerned with reading at the more advanced level required in degree course work: the technique was used to assess history students' awareness of primary and secondary sources and to direct the attention of students of English literature to key features in poems used in a practical criticism exercise. In this section we deal in some detail with only the first of these studies.

Many pupils find difficulty in perceiving a theme or themes in a piece of writing. When a text is presented 'raw' there are several features other than the theme on which readers may naturally focus. If a pupil does not already have the general concept of 'theme' then it will be very difficult for him to recognise a theme in a piece of writing. A verbal description of what is meant by 'a theme' may not be of much help. We were interested to find out if the triplet technique could be used to help to direct attention to themes.

The texts used in our first investigation were three poems. We thought that presenting a poem in a 'triplet' might provide pupils with a context in which the theme was more likely to be recognised. The three poems were so selected that only two of them shared a common theme. One of these poems, however, had content in common with the third poem. Pupils were asked to read the three poems and decide which two 'went together'. We were interested to see whether in this situation pupils would focus on the common content or on the common theme or on some other common feature.

A member of the project team was conducting in-service work on monologue poems with upper secondary classes in a rural comprehensive school. We decided to use some of these poems to construct a 'triplet' to be used with classes which had *not* taken part in the study of monologue. The poems were therefore new to these pupils. Three poems were carefully selected so that two of them shared the same theme. Pupils were not asked to look for common themes, but to select two poems which 'went together in some way'. We hoped that searching for similarities would encourage the pupils to operate at the thematic level. The three poems and the accompanying answer sheet are reproduced as Figures 24 & 25 on pages 154–5.

Poems A and C both have a military background. Poems B and C have a common theme in that the poets, although working in very different contexts, convey the same puzzlement over the injustices of this world. To choose A and C in preference to B and C is to look at the poems at a fairly superficial level, but it cannot be said to be wrong. Once again we come face to face with the problem that in responsive reading we have to allow qualitative differences in responses rather than contrive a situation where we can judge a response as right or wrong.

Sorting or grouping tasks of this kind can vary in the degree of direction imposed. While we were interested in how pupils would sort out these poems, we did have a 'preferred' response pattern. We wanted to see whether the pupils would detect and comment on the shared sense of injustice and ironic quality found in Poems B and C. We assumed that matching A and C because of their common military background would offer an alternative grouping.

Pupils were asked to make two groupings. This emphasised that there are always different ways of looking at texts and, we hoped, might help to encourage flexibility in responding to texts.

The findings

The materials were used initially with a second year mixed ability class in a secondary school. In this section we examine the 'groupings' they made and the ways in which they justified these 'groupings'.

A   **Boots**

We're foot – slog – slog – slog – sloggin' over Africa!
Foot– foot – foot – foot – sloggin' over Africa –
(Boots – boots – boots – boots, movin' up and down again!)
There's no discharge in the war!

Seven – six – eleven – five – nine-an'-twenty mile today –
Four – eleven – seventeen – thirty-two the day before –
(Boots – boots – boots – boots, movin' up and down again!)
There's no discharge in the war!

Don't – don't – don't – don't –look at what's in front of you
(Boots – boots – boots – boots, movin' up an' down again);
Men – men – men – men – men go mad with watchin' 'em,
An' there's no discharge in the war.

Try – try – try – try – to think o' something different –
Oh – my – God – keep – me from goin' lunatic!
(Boots – boots – boots – boots, movin' up an' down again!)
There's no discharge in the war.

B   **Judge Somers**

How does it happen, tell me,
That I who was most erudite of lawyers,
Who knew Blackstone and Coke
Almost by heart, who made the greatest speech
The court-house ever heard, and wrote
A brief that won the praise of Justice Breese –
How does it happen, tell me,
That I lie here unmarked, forgotten,
While Chase Henry, the town drunkard,
Has a marble block, topped by an urn,
Wherein Nature, in a mood ironical,
Has sown a flowering weed?

C   **Tommy Atkins**

I went into a theatre as sober as could be,
They gave a drunk civilian room, but 'adn't none for me;
They sent me to the gallery or round the music-'alls,
But when it comes to fightin, Lord! they'll shove me in the stalls!
For it's Tommy this, an' Tommy that, an'
'Tommy, wait outside';
But it's 'Special train for Atkins' when the
trooper's on the tide,
The troopship's on the tide, my boys, the
troopship's on the tide,
O it's 'Special train for Atkins' when the trooper's
on the tide.

Figure 24:   Triplet Based on Three Poems

Three Poems

1.   Think about the three poems you have just read.

Choose two of the poems which you think 'go together' for some reason, or are alike in some way.

You can choose A & B, or B & C, or A & C.

Write the two letters you chose on this line _____

Now write down why you think they 'go together'.

_____
_____
_____
_____
_____
_____

2.   Think about the three poems again.

Now choose another two that seem to 'go together'.

Write the letters of your new choice here _____

Now write down why you think these two 'go together'.

_____
_____
_____
_____
_____
_____

Figure 25:   Response Sheet for Poetry Triplet

1.   GROUPINGS MADE

The most notable finding was that no pupil grouped Poems A & B.
On the other hand every pupil was able to produce two groupings.
This means that all pupils were able to see some kind of
connection between Poems B & C. This is quite an impressive
finding, epecially since the pupils had not seen these poems before
and were not given any help. (In fact, this was their first
experience of this technique.)

2.   HOW PUPILS JUSTIFIED THEIR GROUPINGS

Pupils justified their groupings in different ways. Only some of
these justifications showed that a common theme had been
recognised. In this section we present an outline of different kinds
of justification offered by pupils. In our discussion we do not
consider whether the pupils' responses were 'right' or 'wrong',
'acceptable' or 'not acceptable'.

(a)   Pointing

In this kind of justification the pupil uses language to 'point' to
elements in the passages. Although a connection is presumably
implied, he or she does not actually produce a statement of that
connection. This pointing approach takes two forms:

(i)   pointing at particulars,
(ii)   retelling, a more elaborate form of pointing which lists
particular elements in sequence.

In the earlier 'preliminary sorting' study with primary school
children, we had found that a number of pupils grouped passages
on the basis of quite specific and narrow features. For example,
they might place passages together because 'water' appeared in
both. This very 'elementary' or even 'crude' level of connection
did *not* appear in the second year pupils' comments on the poems.
Nonetheless justification by mentioning specific features which the
poems had in common was present, although frequently this was
offered to supplement a more general connection. Here is one case
where a pupil points only to a specific connection:

'I think they go together because the first poem is about boots
marching in the first world war and the second poem has

something about a troopship in it.'

This pupil has not produced the more general, military connection and the impression given is that he has not understood, or even studied the poems as wholes.

(b)   Connecting at topic level
At another level of justification the pupil preceives a similarity in content. We have called this 'connecting by topic'. Most pupils saw the *military* connection between Poems A & C and stated it explicitly. In the comment which follows the pupil has identified this common content:

> 'The reasons why I think these poems go together is because they both talk about going to war. Both of them also talk about the troops.'

Some pupils did not make the connection explicit and communality of topic has to be inferred from the details mentioned:

> 'A & C go together because A is about soldiers foot slogging and C is about Tommy Atkins who is also in the army but keeps getting pushed aside.'

Only the 'also' directs the reader to the common topic. Without it there would be nothing to suggest that he was moving beyond 'pointing to specific features'.
Responses in this category were often supplemented by something like the retelling found in the earlier study of passage sorting. Primary pupils sometimes did no more than retell the content as a justification for grouping passages together. The second year secondary pupils also used a form of retelling, but only after the topic connection had been made. Here is an example where the pupil uses direct quotation:

> 'A & C go together because they both deal with the war. Also Tommy says "when it comes to fightin' they'll shove me in the stalls." And the "Boots" poem says "There's no discharge in the war." To come to a conclusion, they all fought in a war

and they'll all be called back when there's another.'

It is not always clear how the 'retelling' or 'quotation' helps connect the passages. As we have already noted 'retelling', in itself, may be regarded as a more elaborate form of 'pointing'.

(c)   Connecting at thematic level
A pupil who identifies the subject matter of a piece of text has identified the topic. When he or she goes on to pinpoint the important things the author has to say about the topic, then the pupil is beginning to consider the theme. It is comparatively easy to connect Poems A & C by topic: it is altogether more difficult to connect them by theme. Indeed, in preparing this triplet, we anticipated that A & C would be connected by topic while B & C would be connected by theme.

In the following comments, pupils first of all identify the common topic and then move on to elucidate common thematic elements:

> 'They go together because they are both about the war. They both tell of the hard work it is and that nobody really cares about how you feel. They also tell that there is only two ways of getting out of the war, either you die or you bear it all until the end of the war.' (Poems A & C)

> 'I think these two go together because the people who do the right things like Judge Somers and Tommy Atkins are not catered for, but Chase Henry, the town drunkard and the drunk civilian get more attention than the other two.' (Poems B & C)

> 'I think that these two go together because in the poems the main characters have worked for their (own?) good and for others but, after a while those that had helped were forgotten and those that had hindered were remembered.' (Poems B & C)

Recognising themes involves generalising beyond the particular context the author has used to carry his ideas.

(d)   Connecting by form, style, etc.

In our preliminary sorting study, some of the primary school pupils grouped passages together because of similarities in style, tone etc. Five second year pupils suggested similarities of this type when grouping Poems A & C. In all cases this was in addition to grouping by topic or theme. One pupil mentioned that 'they both have the same repetitive beat': another suggested that 'they have a sound like a song, with a good rhythm. They also repeat things in them.' This latter feature was described by someone else as follows: 'the words are sometimes said more than once in both poems.' One boy (incorrectly) claimed that 'A & C rhyme while B does not.' Another concluded that both poems were 'written in a funny sort of way.'

3.   POSSIBLE DEVELOPMENTAL TRENDS

We went on to use this triplet with two more groups: a fourth year, 'O' Grade class and a first year undergraduate class studying English literature. We could therefore begin to look for possible developmental trends.

Fourth year pupils differed from second year pupils in that they had a greater tendency to produce multiple connections between texts. They avoided specific connections altogether. They also tended to express thematic connections at a higher level of generality. For example, a fourth year pupil commented:

> 'I think these two go together because they both refer to people who have aimed at doing their best and receive nothing in return for what they have done and other people, such as drunks in the poem, ended up with everything such as the marble block. Strangely, the flowering weed represents the way the drunk would have been when he was alive. Also in the other poem the drunk got a civilian room in the theatre whereas Tommy is only given the gallery or stall.' (Poems B & C)

Note the force of 'such as'.

The undergraduate group operated exclusively at the level of theme and were also much more likely to make reference to stylistic features.

Further Studies Using the Triplet Technique

We carried out three further studies using the triplet technique. One was conducted with secondary school pupils and the texts used were football match reports. Two of the texts were reports of the same game, one a strict chronological account of events and the other a reflective opinion piece. The third passage was again a chronological account but related to a totally different game. All pupils, as expected, grouped the two reports on the same game. More significantly, all of them also grouped together the two chronological passages. It appeared that all pupils had noticed the common stylistic feature though some had difficulty in explaining why they had made this grouping.

It was very noticeable that *none* of these pupils seemed content with the crudest level of specific connection. They all attempted a degree of generalisation. Once again we must emphasise that we are *not* here concerned about whether pupils' interpretations are 'right' or 'wrong'. Our interest is in the *kind* of interpretations they produce.

Two of the additional studies were carried out with undergraduate students. In the first we used history texts to see if students would spontaneously group primary and secondary sources. In the second study the triplet technique was used in an exercise on practical criticism. Undergraduates differed from pupil groups in that they accepted that the similarities they had to look for would be similarities in theme. An alternative was to find similarities in style or form. Many commented on both. No student produced simple similarity of topic, far less similarity through reference to 'particulars'.

The additional information gathered from the studies of fourth year and undergraduate groups gives some support for the analysis of types of justifications drawn up on the evidence provided by the second year group. In particular the absence of 'pointing' and 'retelling' suggests that this level of approach is discarded with increasing maturity.

Note

In this chapter and in the previous one, we have tried to demonstrate that some pupils look at neither the assessment tasks nor the texts themselves in a way that seems 'natural' or 'obvious' to a mature reader. A major concern of formative assessment must be to try to understand the basis on which a pupil is approaching a particular reading task. Part of the hidden curriculum in any subject is learning to recognise what is important in the eyes of subject specialists. Since the subject matter in English teaching is to a large extent presented through text, the ability to pick out what is important or different or significant or novel in a text may be quite fundamental if pupils are to make real progress.

CHAPTER 10

Investigating Pupils' Reading Strategies

In previous chapters, we have been mainly concerned with describing pupils' approaches to selected reading tasks and with searching for common features within broad categories of these tasks. Thus we found that some kinds of problems identified in pupils' handling of dictionaries reappeared when pupils were working with telephone directories. This would be expected because of fundamental similarities between the two kinds of text and similarities between the tasks readers are expected to undertake using them. On the other hand, there are important differences between dictionaries and telephone directories and consequently problems arose in some dictionary tasks for which there were no clear parallels in our work with directories. We would need to work with many more Search-Do reading tasks before we could hope to arrive at a satisfactory description of pupils' difficulties in tackling Search-Do tasks in general.

We must reiterate, however, that these groups of reading tasks were formed only on the basis of the *relative weighting* given to different elements which are present to some degree in all reading tasks. The categories were not mutually exclusive. Pupils might well experience in one kind of task difficulties which were very similar to those uncovered in another kind. For example, in both form-filling (selected as a Comprehend-Do task) and novel-reading (selected as a Comprehend-Personal Response task) we found some pupils who based their answers on information drawn exclusively from personal experience when the type of item they were answering required that they draw on information from the text.

We have tried to produce initial working descriptions of how pupils cope with each category of reading task. Notice, however, that our knowledge has been gained through observing their performance on *reading/assessment* tasks rather than on natural reading tasks. We now present a very speculative outline of the kinds of strategies pupils may adopt when they approach assessment tasks in reading. We begin by considering the pre-requisites for successful and easy handling of such a task.

Pre-requisites for Easy Success in a Reading/Assessment Task

Pupils differ markedly in the amount of effort they are willing or able to devote to a reading/assessment task. Unjust though it may be, there is no necessary correspondence between the amount of effort expended and the degree of success achieved. Throughout the project we found that some pupils succeeded easily while others had to work very hard to produce the same level of performance. Similarly, we came across pupils who struggled very hard but gained little success, while others who failed did so effortlessly. This latter group included pupils who misunderstood the nature of the task that was set. Often their misinterpretation of what they had to do simplified the task so much that they found it easy to produce a response. In effect they were responding to a task quite different from that which faced their companions.

We do not believe that there is one group of pupils which always achieves effortless success, another group which never does and a third which holds an intermediate position. Most pupils experience 'effortless' success in some reading tasks.

In what circumstances is effortless success likely to be achieved? We suggest three conditions. The first two apply to 'natural' reading, and the third is an additional requirement when a supplementary assessment task is set.

1. The reader is already familiar in general terms with the key content of the text used in the reading task. Comprehension is always a constructive process. The reader uses his existing understanding of the concepts and ideas presented by the author to build new ideas and concepts or to form or review attitudes and preconceptions. It is not necessary for the reader

to be completely familiar with the total content of the text. For *ease* of reading, however, the pupil must bring to the text the level of knowledge and experience that the author assumes in his or her readership.

2.. Familiarity with the content of the text is not sufficient in itself. The reader also needs to be familiar with the chosen mode of presentation, not least because this is likely to reflect the author's purpose in writing. Thus the fluent reader recognises and uses the organisational structure in a dictionary entry or a set of directions, the function of the rhetorical devices used by a novelist and the purpose or force of words used symbolically by a poet. The wider and deeper the reader's experience of texts, the more easily he or she can cope with different and unusual presentation formats.

3. Where an assessment task is set there is yet another pre-requisite. The pupil must be familiar with the *kind* of assessment task used. Ideally the assessment task will be congruent with and merge into the reading task itself. This, however, is seldom possible. Teachers have to put pupils into a situation where they have to demonstrate that the reading task has been successfully accomplished. This invariably means making demands of the reader over and above those necessary for successful completion of the natural reading task. An exception to this lies in Comprehend-Do reading where sometimes it may be possible to use completion of the real-life task as a means of assessing the appropriateness of the response. For the most part, however, assessment tasks are not identical to natural reading tasks.

In their own reading, teachers are rarely asked to cope with reading tasks where these three pre-requisites are not met. Certainly, with regard to the material used by their pupils, they know the content, are familiar with the mode of presentation and, as assessors, understand the assessment task and how it is intended to function. When their pupils are assessed through examinations set by others, however, teachers sometimes recognise (and share) the difficulties which can be created by an unfamiliar or inappropriate assessment task. This is particularly the case with external examinations.

When mature adult readers experience difficulty – as may be the case, for example, when they are asked to study complex texts in advanced courses – they find it an uncomfortable experience. Unlike many pupils in schools, however, they have learned how to compensate for weaknesses. They make intelligent guesses to fill gaps in their knowledge, or even rediscover skills in 'waffling'. What they do may, in fact, be no different in purpose or nature from what less competent readers do when faced with apparently easy texts which are nonetheless difficult for them.

In the next few pages we consider the strategies pupils adopt in reading/assessment situations. We are particularly interested in how pupils cope when one or more of these pre-requisites is not met. *All* readers and not just less able readers find themselves in such situations from time to time. Sometimes readers are able to compensate for weaknesses in one or other of the pre-requisites and so arrive at a successful completion of the task. On other occasions the weakness continues to have an adverse effect on the outcome.

To illustrate these strategies we discuss how pupils responded to assessment tasks related to Comprehend-Personal Response reading. We describe three main strategies and argue that each has strengths and weaknesses.

Strategies for Constructing Responses to Assessment Items in Comprehend-Personal Response Tasks

1. *Readers may construct their responses from an internal representation of the content of the text*

If the pre-requisites relating to content and presentation are met, pupils may find it easy to build an internal representation of the content of the text. This internal representation will not retain the exact wording of any section of the text. Rather, it will be a representation of the meaning, tone and attitudes of the text as a whole. If the assessment task is also familiar the total reading/assessment task will appear easy.

Some of the most successful performances on reading/assessment tasks came from those pupils who had attained and used an accurate internal representation of what was in the text. In our work on the novel and on the short story, pupils who gave the fullest explanations for their answers had little need to refer back to the text to refresh their memory, but were able to do so easily when searching for support for their comments.

We suggest, therefore, that most Comprehend-Personal Response assessment tasks assume that the reader has achieved an accurate internal representation of the content of the text. The reader is asked to manipulate ideas and attitudes rather than merely words and sentences. We also hypothesise that readers who are able to do this are more successful even on items which are very specifically tied to particular parts of a text. This is because they are able to find the relevant part of the text more quickly, to relate it to the text as a whole and therefore to interpret it more accurately.

Having attained this kind of internal representation, pupils can 'know', for example, that one character in a novel does not particularly like another, and then recall specific instances to support this contention. They can sensibly discuss the personality and predispositions of a character despite the fact that the amount of direct information any author can give about such matters is very limited.

It is important to recognise, however, that pupils may base their responses on an inaccurate or 'incorrect' internal representation of the content of the text. Results from the 'Pit People' unit and the 'What's Going to Happen?' unit used with 'Pennington's Seventeenth Summer', for example, suggest that some pupils were answering on the basis of inaccurate internal representations. They produced responses which were quite consistent with each other but were not easily reconciled with the actual information given by the author. These pupils seemed to be relying on an internal representation which was built much more on personal experience than on the contents of the text. Their responses therefore tended to be idiosyncratic. For a successful performance readers need to maintain an appropriate balance between two sources of information: the information contained in the text, and the background knowledge and experience they use to interpret it.

2. *Readers may search the text for material on which to build responses*

Where pupils do not attain a very full internal representation of a piece of writing, they may fall back on a *text-based* response strategy. Even for answers to quite general questions they may return to the text and study it carefully. The amount of text the reader is able to reflect on as a single unit has an important influence on the pupil's performance. Pupils using a text-based response strategy are not so likely to integrate information from different parts of the text. Consequently, when reading a novel they may produce fairly simple answers which fail to do justice to the complexity of the issues involved.

We hypothesise that successful text-based responding in reading novels or short stories depends on another factor: the extent to which the sequence of demands in the assessment task mirrors the structure of the text. Where the reader has been able to discern and make use of the structuring in the text and where the assessment task (for example, questioning) has followed this structure closely, then the success rate on the assessment task may be comparable to that of a pupil who is working on a very full and accurate internal reconstruction. The pupil, however, will have had to work very hard on each individual item to achieve success. Success tends to be specific to the item and the reader's understanding is not cumulative. Literal-level questions will be distinctly easier than others and he or she will prefer not to have to draw inferences.

Readers who are unable to discern the structure of the text may be forced to deal with it as a series of barely connected paragraphs or sentences or even words. In these circumstances he or she may have to fall back on background knowledge and experience despite the fact that its inadequacy is the most likely reason for having to adopt a text-based strategy in the first place. Since the text itself does not offer a strong enough context within which to interpret words, phrases and sentences, then personal experience may be called upon to replace it from time to time. This may give a distinctive personal colour to the interpretation of particular parts of the text.

Pupils in this situation are quite likely to become 'stuck' when they come across particular words they do not understand. Pupils they come across particular words they do not understand. Pupils who have a reasonably secure internal representation are less troubled by this: they are better able to fill in gaps through making inferences and are more confident in simply by-passing.

3.   *Readers may use the assessment items as the major source of information on which to build responses*

This strategy is often used when a pupil has attained only limited comprehension of the text. In these circumstances, assessment items themselves become the major source of information used by the pupil to produce responses. Teachers do not intend items to be used in this way. They intend them to stimulate pupils to seek relevant information elsewhere. We found, however, that some pupils can use a strategy which relies heavily on item content as an aid to responding.

When pupils adopt this strategy, their focus is on trying to answer the assessment question, not on trying to understand the text. Sometimes pupils appear to by-pass the text altogether: they answer the questions exclusively from such background knowledge and experience as appears relevant. If there is a degree of passage independence in the question – i.e. if it is answerable without reading and understanding the passage – the responses may well be entirely reasonable. The source of the response, however, is not the text: it is the pupil's pre-existing knowledge. At other times, the pupil may seek an answer from the text despite the fact that he does not understand it. He or she may use low-level features (grammar, signalling devices, wording common to both assessment item and text) and previous experience of the assessment procedure to isolate sections which seem likely to provide answers. While text-based responders may get stuck by a strange word or phrase, question-based responders will *use* this word or phrase in their responses! The answers such pupils produce are frequently incongruous because they have been unable to evaluate them. Nonetheless, considerable effort has gone into arriving at these answers.

Strategies in Reading/Assessment Situations

We have described three broad strategies which pupils might adopt in response to Comprehend-Personal Response assessment tasks. In the first strategy, the reader bases his responses on an internally constructed representation of what is contained in the text. In the second, the reader's responses are based on a more direct search of the text itself. In the third strategy, pupils base their responses to a large extent on the information contained in the questions or assessment items. Three further points are worth making.

First, the descriptions given imply the existence of 'pure' strategies. It was convenient to introduce them in this way. We do not, however, want to suggest that pupils will rely exclusively on any one of these. In practice they are likely to use combinations of these strategies in tackling particular assessment tasks. Thus a pupil may answer some questions on the basis of an internal representation but find that for others it is necessary to adopt a more text-based approach.

Secondly, although the descriptions of these strategies were presented in the context of Comprehend-Personal Response reading, the evidence suggests that the same kind of strategies can be observed when pupils are working on assessment tasks based on other kinds of reading task. For example, in dictionary work some items required integration of a definition with a context. Successful pupils were not constrained by the precise verbal formulation in which the meaning of the word was expressed. They seemed to be able to build their own internal representation of the meaning of the definition. This freed them to experiment with phrasings which could be easily integrated into the source text.

Thirdly, with regard to novel-reading, it might seem logical to ascribe the approach based on internal representation of text content to 'good' readers and the text-based strategy to more modest achievers while reserving the clearly inadequate 'question-based' strategy to the poorest readers. This would be very misleading. There are some kinds of assessment tasks which demand close attention to the exact words used in particular parts of the text. With such items, a text-based strategy will be much more effective than one based on internal representation. The key point is that each of the strategies has strengths and weaknesses. Each can lead to unacceptable responses and yet, in particular circumstances, each can be considered the 'best' approach. In Table 2 we make an attempt to tabulate the strengths and weaknesses of these strategies *as they affect performance in assessment items.*

Table 2:   Characteristics of Different Reading Strategies

Strategy	*Characteristic strengths*	*Characteristic weaknesses*
	Can go beyond the information given.	May read unjustifiable assumptions into the text.
	Answers will usually be in the pupil's own words.	May reveal misinterpretations of the text.
Based on internal representation	Can answer without reference to the text.	Memory for the content of the text may be faulty.
	Sets of answers will usually be internally consistent.	Answers may be consistent but reflect general misinterpretation.
	Allows synthesis of information from different parts of the text.	Interpretation of the text as a whole may colour interpretation of individual sections of it.
	Will usually be able to provide an answer.	May not really answer the questions asked.

Strategy	Characteristic strengths	Characteristic weaknesses
	Answers will largely use the words of the text and therefore will be accurate in that sense.	May not be able to give a valid interpretation of the words used. May get stuck at unknown words even if they are irrelevant for the task.
Text-based	Will rarely go beyond the information given in the text to make unjustifiable assumptions. Performs well at literal level.	Insecure on inferential questions which demand thinking beyond the text.
	Answers will tend to focus on the relevant parts of the text.	Will be less successful with questions which demand synthesis of information drawn from diverse parts of the text.
	Will use the wording or the question (and/or parts of the text) to formulate answers.	Answers result from puzzle-solving rather than from comprehension of the text.
Question-based	Will try to produce an answer (even if the question and/or the text are not understood).	Answers bear only surface connection with the text and may be incongruous.

Competent performance on reading/assessment tasks requires a judicious use of all three approaches. Different categories of reading tasks may require a different balance of strategies. Reading a novel seems a clear-cut instance where building an internal representation of the content of the task is essential. Yet this interpretation must remain in contact with the text. If it does not, the characteristic weaknesses of the strategy as listed in Table 2 will come into play. Formative assessment tasks may have the effect of bringing the reader back into contact with the text.

The characteristic weaknesses of strategies based on internal representations make it less appropriate in Comprehend-Do situations. The strengths of the text-based strategy match the demands made by such tasks rather well. The dispensing of medicines, for example, demands systematic reference to the text.

Question-based response strategies may be regarded as an artefact of assessment tasks. Adequate attention to the question or item is necessary in any assessment situation. The strengths of the strategy are not negligible, however, for they match some of the elementary requirements of Search-Do tasks. The strategy is frequently used when a reading-assessment task is too difficult for the pupils. In these circumstances it may be the only strategy available to them. The alternative is simply to give up.

Implications for Formative Assessment

A reading/assessment task seldom corresponds exactly with the natural reading task. When this does occur we may be able to observe the reader interacting directly with the text. In all other circumstances our view is going to be obstructed or coloured by an intervening assessment task. In the previous section we offered some hypotheses as to the ways in which pupils may arrive at their responses.

Since assessment tasks seldom match closely with natural reading tasks, problems for assessment arise at all stages of reading development. In primary school, reading is often assessed by listening to a child's oral rendering of the text. A perfect performance may be produced by a child who has understood little or given only scant attention to meaning. Oral reading is *assumed* to reflect an ability to understand. A similar situation arises in higher education. Ability to write an essay about 'Macbeth' is assumed to demonstrate ability to comprehend and appreciate the text. Yet it is not unknown for students who have never actually read the play to produce satisfactory examination answers. In this case the mismatch between the assessment task and the natural reading task is so great that it is difficult to see how it can plausibly be defended. At higher education level the ability to read the text is assumed. In conducting this project, however, we have learned to question assumptions of this kind.

There must always be doubts about the validity of drawing conclusions about a pupil's reading of a text from his or her performance on appended assessment tasks. Given this situation, the teacher can only try to match the pupil, the text and the reading/assessment task. The aim must be to construct questions and exercises in such a way that, as far as possible, they invoke the same processes as are demanded by the natural reading task. The greater the degree of fit between assessment task and reading task the more confident they can be about gaining genuine formative information.

Teachers, then, must bear two points in mind. Firstly, success or failure on an assessment task does not always indicate success or failure on the reading task involved. Secondly, teaching must be directed towards success in *reading tasks*, not assessment tasks. When the reading and assessment tasks are inadequately matched, information gained will not reflect pupils' reading performance and subsequent teaching may be misdirected.

CHAPTER 11

Developing an Assessment Resource

Underlying the approach and procedures described in this report are several recurrent ideas and assumptions. In this chapter we review these.

1. *The reading curriculum*

Our initial analysis of the materials sent to us by schools showed that pupils are expected to cope with a very wide range of reading activities. We devised the Framework described in Chapter 1 to group these reading activities into categories of reading tasks. The framework proved to be useful and it is for this reason, rather than because of any proven validity as an analysis of reading tasks, that it has remained unchanged throughout the project.

2. *Reading tasks*

In adopting this approach we did not try to classify reading tasks into neat, mutually exclusive categories. It seemed to us that reading tasks were best differentiated in terms of the relative weighting given to certain basic elements (Search, Comprehend, Personal Response, Learn/Store and Do). The framework assumes that all reading tasks can be analysed in terms of these five elements. Some reading tasks involve all of them with one or two perhaps playing only a very minor role. Other reading tasks may involve fewer elements. Individual elements, then, have a relatively high weighting in some tasks but are insignificant or absent in others. Seen in this way, the framework functions as a kind of sampling guide. It can be used to ensure that when we study a pupil's reading we look at how he performs across a representative sample of reading tasks. For example, a pupil may be comparatively weak in the detailed interpretation of short passages but substantially more successful in reading novels.

3.   *Investigating specific reading tasks*

In the case of specific reading tasks, our approach was to produce assessment materials which would readily elicit initial responses. In each study we found it necessary to move beyond the pupil's original response to ask for explanations and justifications. This was true even in those investigations where we made the greatest effort to produce polished questions which, we hoped, would produce unambiguous responses. The literature on questioning is full of attempts to provide teachers with means of producing 'good' questions. While fully accepting the need to prepare questions of high quality, we doubt whether such questions in themselves always provide formative information. In setting out to prepare 'very good' questions one presupposes that there is a desirable or logically correct answer. Questioning is then directed at securing that answer. However, there needs to be a degree of 'openness' in questions if the thinking which underlies a pupil's spontaneous responses is to be revealed. On the other hand, while open questions give pupils more freedom to respond, their use often makes it impossible to decide whether pupils' problems derive from difficulties in reading the text or from difficulties in formulating a response to the questions. We found that for formative assessment purposes a comparatively closed question, which readily elicited a first response, followed by a request for an explanation of that response was a successful combination.

The 'logic' by which pupils produce responses often becomes clear only when their interpretation of the task is understood or when the limited sources on which they have based their responses are recognised. Understanding the logic by which pupils arrive at an inappropriate response is probably the most important step in preparing to help them.

4.   *Techniques for constructing items*

The aim of the project was to help teachers in the preparation of their own assessment materials rather than to provide them with ready made items or assessment units. We devised a range of possible techniques for constructing such materials. Merely providing a collection of techniques does *not*, however, constitute a formative assessment resource. To think in such terms is to suffer from the 'illusion of technique' (Barrett, 1979). Formative information is gained through the interpretation of pupils' responses to assessment materials. This is why we have stressed that the most important element in any assessment resource is the acquisition of information leading to a deeper understanding and appreciation of the nature of reading tasks and the difficulties inherent in them. Since gathering this kind of information is a cumulative process teachers must see the maintenance of formative assessment resources as an ongoing activity.

Of considerable importance is the extent to which a technique, used successfully in the study of one task, can be applied to other similar tasks and further refined and extended through studies of these. There will, of course, always be a need to consider whether a given technique *should* be applied to other texts and tasks. If, however, a technique is found to be inappropriate for use with another text this should not automatically be seen as a weakness in the technique. It may be an indication that significant differences exist between the texts and that the range of techniques needs to be broadened.

5.   *Investigating reading strategies*

For each category of reading task, we carried out at least two investigations. These studies, carried out *within* categories, enabled us to identify common sources of difficulty and to describe some of the strategies pupils adopted in trying to overcome their difficulties. Since, however, our categories of reading task were not mutually exclusive, we also found instances where the same sources of difficulty appeared *across* tasks selected from different categories of reading task: for example, difficulties in deciding what features of a text should be attended to or difficulties arising from imperfect understanding of the structure of a text.

In each of our investigations the most useful information was provided by pupils who had experienced some difficulty with the assessment task. We were often able to identify where the 'strategies' of such pupils' proved inadequate. For example, they often failed to make use of sources of information which were ostensibly available to them. Nonetheless, their responses in such circumstances were not random; their way of proceeding had some direction. Whether or not this constitutes a strategy needs not only agreement over the definition of 'strategy' (see, for example, van Dijk & Kintsch, 1983) but also further study of the more positive features of the approaches adopted by pupils. At the moment we have suggested three broad strategies each of which has strengths and weaknesses which make it appropriate in some contexts and inappropriate in others. It is important to realise that pupils' reading strategies cannot usually be inferred from their performances on natural reading tasks but have to be inferred (as we have done) from their responses in reading/assessment tasks. The closer the match between the natural reading task and the assessment task set, the more valid such inferences are likely to be.

The aim of this project was to provide help for teachers conducting that kind of informal assessment which enhances responsiveness to pupils' needs in day-to-day teaching. What has been produced is not an item bank nor even an item collection (although some of our techniques could be used to produce items for such a bank or collection). Instead we have tried to gather together, and organise within a framework based on reading tasks, two kinds of information:

> information relating to the difficulties pupils have with different reading tasks and the strategies pupils use in tackling them;

> information about how teachers may construct assessment materials to help them to investigate the difficulties particular pupils are experiencing.

In this way we have attempted to lay the foundations of an assessment resource which teachers can use and develop to meet the needs of their own pupils.

APPENDIX 1

Project Working Papers

1. FYFE, R. & NORTHCROFT, D.J. Framework for the Assessment Resource.
2. MITCHELL, E. & McPHILLIMY, W.N. Search-Do Reading: (1) Using a Telephone Directory.
3. MITCHELL, E. & FYFE, R. Comprehend-Do Reading: (1) Reading Instructions.
4. FYFE, R., MITCHELL, E. & McPHILLIMY, W.N. The Assessment of Reading Comprehension: A Survey of Techniques.
5. FYFE, R., MITCHELL, E., McPHILLIMY, W.N. & NORTHCROFT, D.J. Formative Assessment of Novel Reading: (1) Introduction to Assessment Techniques.
6. FYFE, R., MITCHELL, E. & McPHILLIMY, W.N. Comprehend-Do Reading: (2) Filling in a Booking Form.
7. MITCHELL, E. Cloze Procedure – A Review of the Literature.
8. DUTCH, R. A Survey of Profile Systems.
9. NORTHCROFT, D.J. Pupils' Responses to Literature: A Review of the Literature.
10. FYFE, R. & MITCHELL, E. Formative Assessment of Novel Reading: (2) Report on 'Pit Country' Unit.
11. FYFE, R. & MITCHELL, E. Formative Assessment of Novel Reading: (3) Report on 'Pit Story' Unit.
12. FYFE, R. & MITCHELL, E. Formative Assessment of Novel Reading: (4) Report on 'Pit People' Unit.
13. MITCHELL, E. Formative Assessment of Novel Reading: (5) Report on 'Butch in Court' Unit.
14. FYFE, R., MITCHELL, E., CUNNINGHAM, D.C. & McPHILLIMY, W.N. Formative Assessment of Novel Reading: (6) General Applicability of Techniques.
15. FYFE, R., CUNNINGHAM, D.C. & MITCHELL, E. Reading a Short Story: (1) Introduction to Assessment Techniques.
16. FYFE, R., MITCHELL, E. & CUNNINGHAM, D.C. Recognising Kinds of Text: (1) Passage Sorting.
17. MITCHELL, E. & McPHILLIMY, W.N. Comprehend-Do Reading: (3) Filling in an Application Form.

18. FYFE, R. & CUNNINGHAM, D.C. Recognising Kinds of Text: (2) The Triplet Technique.
19. CUNNINGHAM, D.C. Formative Assessment and the Nature of Fiction.
20. MITCHELL, E. Search-Do Reading: (2) Using a Dictionary – a Preliminary Analysis.
21. MITCHELL, E. Search-Do Reading: (3) Difficulties in Using a Dictionary.
22. NORTHCROFT,   D.J.   Pupils'   Responses   to Literature: Implications for Classroom Teaching.
23. FYFE, R., CUNNINGHAM, D.C. & MITCHELL, E. Reading a Short Story: (2) Report on 'History Lesson' Materials.
24. FYFE, R., CUNNINGHAM, D.C. & MITCHELL, E. Formative Assessment of Novel Reading: (7) Report on 'Boats and Music' Unit.

APPENDIX 2

Copyright Materials: Acknowledgements

In this document we have reproduced only a handful of the texts which were actually used in the project. The sources of these texts have been included in the list of acknowledgements (p.ix). Many more texts were used in preparing for and carrying out the individual investigations. We would like to acknowledge the help of individuals and companies who allowed us to reproduce copyright material for use in the project.

The following companies gave us permission to use sets of instructions from their products in our studies of Comprehend-Do Reading:

Askit Laboratories Ltd.

Beecham Group Ltd.

Bees Ltd.

Berger, Jenson & Nicholson
  Ltd.

Care Laboratories (I.C.I.)

Carters Tested Seeds Ltd.

Goodlass Wall & Co. Ltd.

W.W. Johnson & Son Ltd.

Merck Sharpe & Dohme Ltd.

Miles Laboratories Ltd.

Arthur Sanderson & Sons Ltd.

W. Smith & Son Ltd.

Smith & Walton Ltd.

Sterling-Winthrop Group Ltd.

Suttons Seeds Ltd., Torquay

Thompson & Morgan (Ipswich)
  Ltd.

Unwins Seeds Ltd.

The following companies allowed us to use their materials in our studies of form-filling:

Anglia Holidays Ltd.

Butlin's Ltd.

Comet Radiovision Services
  Ltd.

Driver & Vehicle Licensing
Centre, Swansea
Golden Rail Holidays

Hotelplan (Inghams Travel)
Thomson Travel Ltd.
Wings Ltd.

The following authors gave us permission to quote from their work in investigations of Comprehend-Personal-Response Reading: Michael Hamburger, William McIlvanney, Mrs Anne Ridler and Ian Serraillier.

The following publishers and authors' agents gave us permission to quote from published work in several of our studies:

The Bodley Head
Bolt & Watson Ltd.
Collins Publishers Ltd.
Encyclopaedia Britannica International Ltd.
Faber & Faber Ltd.
Harrap Ltd.
Heinemann Educational Books
Hodder & Stoughton Children's Books
Hutchinson Publishing Group
Ladybird Books Ltd.
Lutterworth Press
Macmillan Education Ltd.
Methuen London Ltd.
Michael Joseph Ltd.
Oxford University Press
Penguin Books Ltd.
Scholastic Publications Ltd.
Van Nostrand Reinhold Co. Ltd.
Frederick Warne Ltd.
A. Wheaton & Co. Ltd.

References

ANDERSON, R.C. & FREEBODY, P. (1979). *Vocabulary Knowledge*. Technical Report No. 136. University of Illinois: Center for the Study of Reading.

ANDERSON, R.C. & SHIFRIN, Z. (1980). 'The meaning of words in context'. In: SPIRO, R.J., BRUCE, B.C. & BREWER, W.F. (Eds) (1980): *Theoretical Issues in Reading Comprehension*. Hillsdale, N.J.: Lawrence Erlbaum Associates.

BARRETT, T.C. (1968). 'Cognitive and affective dimensions of reading comprehension'. Reprinted in MELNIK, A. & MERRITT, J. (Eds) (1972) *Reading: Today and Tomorrow*. University of London Press, pp.56–60.

BARRETT, W. (1979). *The Illusion of Technique*. Wm. Kimber.

BARSTOW, S. (1960). *A Kind of Loving*. Michael Joseph.

BECK, I., McKEOWN, M.G., McCASLIN, E.S. & BURKES, A.M. (1978). *Instructional Dimensions that may affect Reading Comprehension*. University of Pittsburgh: Learning Research and Development Center.

BRUCE, B.C. & NEWMAN, D. (1978) 'Interacting Plans'. *Cognitive Science*, 2, 195–233.

CLARKE, A.C. (1954). *Expedition to Earth*. Sidgwick & Jackson.

DAVIS, F.B. (1968) 'Research in comprehension in reading'. *Reading Research Quarterly*, 3, 499–545.

DAVIS, F.B. (1972). 'Psychometric research on comprehension in reading'. *Reading Research Quarterly*, 7, 628–678.

GERHARD, C. (1975). *Making Sense*. Newark, Delaware: International Reading Association.

GUSZAK, F. (1972). *Diagnostic Reading Instruction in the Elementary School*. New York: Harper & Row.

HENRY, G.H. (1974). *Teaching Reading as Concept Development*. Newark, Delaware: International Reading Association.

HOGABOAM, T. & PERFETTI, C. (1975). 'Lexical ambiguity & sentence comprehension.' *Journal of Verbal Learning & Verbal Behavior* 14, 265–274.

JOHNSTON, P.H. (1983). *Reading Comprehension Assessment: A Cognitive Basis*. Newark, Delaware: International Reading Association.

LUNZER, E. & GARDNER, K. (Eds) (1979). *The Effective Use of Reading.* Heinemann Educational Books for the Schools Council.

MADDOCK, R. (1969). *The Pit.* Macmillan Education Ltd.

MASON, J., KNISELY, E. & KENDALL, J. (1979). 'Effects of polysemous words on sentence comprehension'. *Reading Research Quarterly* Vol.15, No.1, 49–65.

MITCHELL, E. (1983). *Search-Do Reading: (2) Using a Dictionary – a Preliminary Analysis.* Formative Assessment of Reading Strategies in Secondary Schools, Working Paper 20. Aberdeen College of Education.

PEYTON, K.M. (1970). *Pennington's Seventeenth Summer.* Oxford University Press.

POPHAM, W. (1981). *Modern Educational Measurement.* Prentice-Hall.

REED, G.F. (1968). Skill. In LUNZER, E.A. & MORRIS, J.F. (Eds) (1968). *Development in Learning, Vol.2:   Development in Human Learning.* Staples Press.

SATTERLY, D. (1981). *Assessment in Schools.* Oxford: Basil Blackwell.

SCHANK, R.C. & ABELSON, R.P. (1977). *Scripts, plans, goals and understanding.* Hillsdale, N.J.: Lawrence Erlbaum Associates.

S.E.D. (1977a). *Assessment for All.* Edinburgh: H.M.S.O.

S.E.D. (1977b). *The Structure of the Curriculum in the Third and Fourth Years of the Scottish Secondary School.* Edinburgh: H.M.S.O.

S.E.D. (1981). *The Munn and Dunning Reports: the Government's Development Programme. Syllabus and Assessment Guidelines: English, Foundation Level.* Edinburgh: Scottish Education Department.

SINGER, H. & DONLAN, D. (1982). 'Active comprehension: problem-solving schema with question generation for comprehension of complex short stories'. *Reading Research Quarterly,* Vol.17, (2), 166–186.

SPEARITT, D. (1972). 'Identification of reading comprehension by maximum likelihood factor analysis'. *Reading Research Quarterly,* 8, 92–111.

STAUFFER, R.G. (1971). 'Thorndike's "Reading as reasoning": a perspective'. *Reading Research Quarterly,* 6, 443–448.

STEINBERG, C. & BRUCE, B.C. (1980). 'Higher-level features in children's stories: Rhetorical structure and conflict'. In: KAMIL, M.L. & MOE, A.J. (Eds). *Perspectives in reading research and instruction,* 117–125. Washington D.C.: National Reading Conference.

STICHT, T. (1977). 'Comprehending reading at work'. In: JUST, M.A. & CARPENTER, P.A. (Eds) (1977). *Cognitive Processes in Comprehension.* U.S.A.: Lawrence Erlbaum.

SULZBY, E. (1980). 'Word concept development activities'. In: HENDERSON, E.H. & BEERS, J.W. (Eds) (1980). *Developmental and Cognitive Aspects of Learning to Spell.* Newark, Delaware: International Reading Association.

THORNDIKE, E.L. (1917). 'Reading as reasoning: a study of mistakes in paragraph reading'. *Journal of Educational Psychology,* 8, 6, 323–332.

THORNDIKE, R.L. (1974). 'Reading as reasoning'. *Reading Research Quarterly*, 9, 137–147.

van DIJK, T.A. & KINTSCH, W. (1983). *Strategies of Discourse Comprehension*. Academic Press.

VYGOTSKY, L.S. (1978). *Mind in Society: The Development of Higher Psychological Processes*. Harvard University Press.

WRIGHT, P. (1980). 'Strategy and tactics in the design of forms'. *Visible Language*, 14, 2, 151–193.

Index